Walks with God

Daily Exercise for the Journey to Heaven

Edwin Crozier

DeWard
for your journey

Walks with God: Daily Exercise for the Journey to Heaven
© 2015 by DeWard Publishing Company, Ltd.
P.O. Box 6259, Chillicothe, Ohio 45601
800.300.9778
www.deward.com

Cover design by Jonathan Hardin.

Unless otherwise noted, scripture quotations are taken from The Holy Bible, English Standard Version®, copyright ©2001 by Crossway Bibles, a publishing ministry of Good News Publishers. Used by permission. All rights reserved.

Scriptures marked NASU, are taken from the New American Standard Bible ®, Copyright © 1960, 1962, 1963, 1968, 1971, 1972, 1973, 1975, 1977, 1995 by the Lockman Foundation. Used by permission.

Any emphasis in Bible quotations is added.

Reasonable care has been taken to trace original sources for any excerpts and quotations appearing in this book and to document such information. For material not in the public domain, fair-use standards and practices were followed. Should any attribution be found to be incorrect or incomplete, the publisher welcomes written documentation supporting correction for subsequent printings.

Printed in the United States of America.

ISBN: 978-1-936341-75-7

Gratitude

Thanks to God who has given me the ability to study, the time to write and the opportunity to share my faith with others. My prayer is that He is glorified by this book.

Thank you, Marita for putting up with me while I write, especially when the deadlines are coming and I leave you to do all the work at home. You are the best wife I could have.

Thanks to the Franklin Church of Christ in Franklin, Tenn., who always gets to be the guinea pig for all my ideas and all my writing. You are always so supportive and encouraging. I would never be able to write these books without your loving words.

Special thanks to Phillip Shumake and Michelle Alford. Phillip, you went above and beyond the call of duty to help me not only with the cover of the original version of this book, but the icons, the layout and the format. Michelle, you read through the manuscript and didn't even complain that you were rushed because I was behind schedule. Thanks guys.

Also By
EDWIN CROZIER

Books:

Plugged In: High Voltage Prayer

Built By the Lord: A Study of the Family

The Gospel of the Kingdom: Studies in the Sermon on the Mount

Give Attention to Reading

DVD:

Your First 10 Days as a Christian

Walks With God
Table of Contents

Warming Up for the Journey

Thus says the Lord: "Let not the wise man boast in his wisdom, let not the mighty man boast in his might, let not the rich man boast in his riches, but let him who boasts boast in this, that he understands and knows me, that I am the Lord who practices steadfast love, justice, and righteousness in the earth. For in these things I delight, declares the Lord."

Jeremiah 9.23-24

A friend of mine went to high school with Brad Paisley. Another played football against Troy Aikman in high school. Another lives next door to the lead guitarist of *Chicago*. When people travel to Franklin, Tennessee, one of our favorite pastimes is showing them the houses of the famous people that live here. I love to tell people I flew on a plane with Deborah Harry, lead singer of Blondie, I said "Hi" to Amy Grant (even if it was from a distance of 10 feet while she talked to someone else and didn't even notice me), I passed Michael W. Smith on my way out of Lowe's once and I actually had a brief conversation with John Maxwell. I especially like to show people my picture with Kenneth Starr, however, half the time I have to tell them who Kenneth Starr is.

Let's face it. We love to let people know about our brushes with fame. It is as if we think a little bit of the importance rubs off on us. How awesome it would be if we could actually be friends with someone famous and important. What if we could walk with them, talk with them and spend time with them?

Actually, we can. We can have that relationship with someone immanently more famous and important than any television star, singer or politician. I know we cannot see Him, touch Him or even have a verbal conversation with Him. However, we can have a relationship. We can know His presence, comfort and peace. We can walk with God. **Hebrews**

13.5 says, "Be content with what you have, for he has said, 'I will never leave you nor forsake you.'"[1]

The Bible describes two people that walked with God. "Enoch walked with God, and he was not, for God took him."[2] "Noah was a righteous man, blameless in his generation. Noah walked with God."[3]

Wouldn't you like to be on the list of walkers with God? Look at the blessings these two received. In a list of people who died, Enoch stood out. He didn't die, but was taken. In an earth of people lost in the flood, Noah survived because he walked with God. Sure, it is neat to fly on a plane with a singer, shake hands with a self-help guru and get a picture taken with a star prosecutor. None of this, however, compares with the blessings of walking with God every day.

In the 1990 acclaimed film, *Dances with Wolves*, Lt. Dunbar, played by Kevin Costner, was assigned to a deserted western frontier post. He befriended a wolf. The Indians in the area saw him playing with the wolf and named him "Dances With Wolves." Wouldn't it be great if we lived in such a way that they would have called us "Walks With God"?

That is what this little book is about—walking with God. Every day thousands of Christians hit the gym, go for a run, take a swim or practice Pilates. We want to take care of our bodies so they will be around for a while. Regrettably, too many are missing out on the greatest exercise of all—walking with God. It is good for the heart, good for the soul, and, yes, it is even good for the body. It is the only exercise with everlasting benefits. This book is like an exercise manual, helping you get in shape spiritually and lay aside the burdens that entangle you.

If we are going to walk with God, we must get to know Him. There is only one way to do that. Get into His Word and learn what He says about Himself.

This book is a tool to help you develop your daily walk with God, designed to have daily readings every weekday for five weeks. Each reading is divided into two sections.

Getting Our Bearings   *Hand in Hand*

---

1   When I am writing, I capitalize pronouns referring to deity. However, when I quote from the Bible, I will use the format of the translation I am quoting. The only exception is I do not capitalize all the letters of "Lord" when it interprets the tetragrammaton.
2   **Genesis 5.24**
3   **Genesis 6.9**

The first will address the nature of God proclaimed in the Bible. The second will provide practical advice for walking with God today based on who and what He is. Feel free to read them together or to divide them into two daily walks with God.

One side of walking with God is meeting Him and listening to Him through His Word. The other side is talking to Him through prayer. At the end of each day's reading, I have included an outline to help you build your own prayer based on what you have learned in the reading.[4]

Also, at the end of each week's readings is a group discussion to help you walk with God's other children as well.

Many Christians can look at the map and discuss directions. They check the distances between points A, B and C and they examine the topography. But walking with God is different from merely examining His map. It is one thing to make note of a mountain on a map; it is another to climb it. It is one thing to examine a stream on a chart; it is another to ford it. We may know the maps very well, but the blessings do not come to those who read the maps. They come to those who climb the mountains and ford the streams.

Make your commitment now to walk with God. Find others with whom you can walk. Whether you have been on the journey for a long time, are just starting or need to get back on track, let this study draw you closer to God. If you stick with it, when this month is over, I guarantee you will be closer to God, stronger in the faith and further in your journey to heaven.

May God richly bless you as you draw closer to Him. More importantly, may you richly bless God.

---

4   If you do not know how to fill out the outline for building your prayer, read the Appendix on page 225.

Week One
The Powerful God

"In the beginning, God created the heavens and the earth."
Genesis 1.1

1

In the Beginning, God...

Getting Our Bearings

"In the beginning, God..."[5]

Genesis' initial readers needed no further proof. After all, they saw the plagues on Egypt. They crossed the Red Sea on dry land. They saw the waters crash down on Pharaoh's army. They witnessed the lightening and heard the thunder on Mt. Sinai. They gazed on Moses' shining face. They drank water from the rock and ate manna from heaven. They wandered in the wilderness while their shoes refused to wear out and their feet did not swell. They watched as the ground opened up and swallowed Korah, Dathan and Abiram. They witnessed the cloud of smoke by day and the pillar of fire by night.

We, perhaps, need a little more help. We did not see the signs, marvel at the miracles or witness the wonders. We read of God's direct encounters with Abraham, Moses and Paul and wonder why we do not have more sure signs. Yet, all we really need is right here in **Genesis 1.1**. Not that the verse itself is proof of God. Rather, it provides the best explanation for why there are heavens and earth.

Christians and naturalists alike know there are heavens and earth and both ask how. Sadly, the naturalists have tampered with the rules, and, therefore, they cannot answer the question. They claim no matter what we say about why we are here, we are not allowed to suggest a supernatural explanation. Thus, no matter what evidence is found, they have to fit it into a godless model.

Our universe is governed by laws. One of which is called the Law of Conservation. Essentially, this law claims the total amount of energy and matter in the universe remains constant. It may change forms, but energy and matter do not come into existence or go out of existence.

Thus, if only our natural system exists, the energy and matter have always been here. The heavens and earth did not come into existence; they always existed (in one form or another).

However, a second law is called the Law of Entropy. This law essentially says everything winds down. Like a spinning top, no matter how hard you spin it, it eventually winds down and stops. No top can spin forever. Our heavens and earth are like a spinning top—winding down. The problem? According to our first law, the heavens have been here forever. That means they have been winding down forever. However, no top can spin forever. Thus, the second law says our heavens had to come into existence at some point.

If all we have is our natural universe, we have a severe problem. One law tells us the heavens have always been here. The other says it must have started at some point. What is the answer?

"In the beginning, God..."

Think of what this means about God. The laws of our universe do not bind Him. Two objects cannot occupy the same space at the same time—except for God. For every action there is an equal and opposite reaction—not with God. Time marches on—not for God. Stop for a moment and be amazed at the God who created the laws and is bound by none. He brought matter and energy into existence from nothing. He started time. He initiated inertia. Gravity cannot ground Him. Electrical currents do not charge Him. Time does not change Him.

We are not surprised when the angel told Mary, "Nothing will be impossible with God."[6] Nor are we surprised when Paul explained God is able "to do far more abundantly beyond all that we ask or think."[7] This is the God we adore, "the Alpha and the Omega...who is and who was and who is to come, the Almighty."[8] He is not the source of power. He is power. We must not forget it.

Think About It:

Has there been any problem in your life about which you have thought God could do nothing? List it below and then pray about it, right now.

---

6   Luke 1.37
7   Ephesians 3.20, NASB
8   Revelation 1.8

Hand in Hand

Before we learn anything about how the beginning impacts our daily walk with God, let's simply be in awe of His majesty. "The Lord is in his holy temple. Let all the earth keep silence before him."⁹ Be in awe and meditate on God's greatness.

As you consider that greatness, remember what Solomon said about God in **I Kings 8.23, 27**:

> O Lord, God of Israel, there is no God like you, in heaven above or on earth beneath...But will God indeed dwell on the earth? Behold, heaven and the highest heaven cannot contain you; how much less this house that I have built.

Solomon understood God is not bound by our universe. His existence cannot be contained within the realm of the physical and material. No box bounds our God. In like manner, no box of human construction can contain the character and nature of God.

Voltaire allegedly said, "If God created us in his own image, we have more than reciprocated." Sadly, this is true. Too many are not walking with the God that is, they are walking with the god they have created in their own mind. Even sadder, many are trying to avoid the god they have created in their own mind.

If we are going to walk with God, we must know Him as He is, not as we imagine Him to be or even want Him to be. We cannot make boxes for Him.

Consider some of the boxes people have made. "The great God who created the universe must be demanding and exacting. I could never do enough to serve Him and He could never forgive me. All that New Testament teaching about grace just can't apply to me." Or consider another. "God is a god of love. All that judgment in the Old Testament just can't be real. The real God would never do that."

Folks who develop these boxes are like the Jews and Greeks of **I Corinthians 1.22-24**:

For Jews demand signs and Greeks seek wisdom, but we preach Christ crucified, a stumbling block to the Jews and folly to the Gentiles, but to those who are called, both Jews and Greeks, Christ the power of God and the wisdom of God.

The Jews could fathom God appearing in the form of man. However, the Son of God living as a man and then dying? No way. Despite the clear message of **Isaiah 53**, that concept just didn't fit in their box. Therefore, they were oblivious to the great sign of the resurrection.[10] The Greeks could fathom the gods walking among them. They even had stories of gods who died and lived again. However, a God who died as a sacrifice to save men? No way. To the Greeks, gods demanded sacrifices, they didn't become them. That was just foolish. They created boxes for God and when He didn't fit their boxes, they turned away. We must not make the same mistake.

If we will walk hand in hand with God, we must get rid of our boxes. We must not be surprised that He doesn't fit within them. Think about this. If the god you believe in fits neatly within the box you have created in your mind, then he is likely nothing more than a creation of your mind.

The God who doesn't think like us, whose ways are higher than ours as the heavens are higher than the earth,[11] is going to act in some surprising ways. We are going to read passages that shock us. We are going to endure situations that surprise us. Just look at Job. He and his friends had created a box for God. Their box said God only let bad things happen to bad people. When bad things happened to Job, his friends assumed he had been a bad man. Job assumed God was being unfair. In the end, God's answer was essentially, "I am God and you are not." Job responded, "Therefore I have uttered what I did not understand, things too wonderful for me, which I did not know."[12]

When all is said and done, if we are going to walk with God, we must get to know Him as He is based on how He has revealed Himself through His Word. We will certainly be surprised. We will find things that puzzle us. We may, at times, even learn things that seem contradictory. Let's not be surprised. Our finite minds simply cannot fathom the infinite, unbounded nature of God.

Before you get frustrated with this, think in these terms. Do you really want to walk with a god that is limited by what man can think and fathom? Or do you want to walk with the God who caused the beginning.

---

10   **Cf. Romans 1.4**
11   **Isaiah 55.8-9**
12   **Job 42.3**

Think About It:
What boxes have people created for God?

What boxes have you created for God?

How can you get rid of these?

Praying to Our God

Dear God, You are…

Dear God, You…

Dear God, thank You…

Dear God, forgive me for…

Dear God, help me…

2

God, The Creator

Getting Our Bearings

"In the beginning, God created..."[13]

I do not believe any book starts as powerfully as **Genesis** and, therefore, the Bible. The Bible is God's story, His autobiography. The very first thing God tells us about Himself is He is Creator.

God created. He did not form. He did not fashion. He did not organize. He did not mold. He created. **Genesis 1.2** says, "The earth was without form and void, and darkness was over the face of the deep," but do not misunderstand this verse. As we learned in the last chapter, God is not telling us He merely molded pre-existing matter and energy into our universe. Rather, God brought the heavens and earth into existence from nothing. His first creative act was to bring into existence a formless, void earth covered in darkness. He then proceeded to fashion the universe for the remainder of the creation week.

There was nothing, then by God's power there was something. But why? Why did God create? Perhaps it is impossible to drill down to one overarching answer to this question. However, I believe we can find a good explanation in Scripture.

God did not create because He had to. He was not a lonely God in need of companionship. As He said in **Psalm 50.12**, "If I were hungry, I would not tell you, for the world and all its fullness is mine." God did not create because He needed to, but because He wanted to.

Further, notice Paul's summary of the creation in **Colossians 1.16-17**: For by him all things were created, in heaven and on earth, visible and invisible, whether thrones or dominions or rulers or authorities—all things were created through him and for him. And he is before all things, and in him all things hold together.

All things were not only created through Him, but for Him. The creation is not for us. It is for God. Don't misunderstand. God's creation does say a great deal about His love for us. However, the primary purpose behind creation was for God, not us. We must not lift ourselves up but remember our place. God is the pre-eminent one. We are the creature. He is the Creator.

Finally, note **Isaiah 43.7**: "...everyone who is called by name, whom I created for my glory, whom I formed and made." Why did God create? He did so for His glory.

The heavens declare the glory of God, and the sky above proclaims his handiwork. Day to day pours out speech, and night to night reveals knowledge. There is no speech, nor are there words, whose voice is not heard. Their voice goes out through all the earth and their words to the end of the world.[14]

We, the pinnacle of God's creation, have also been created to glorify God. In fact, fulfilling that mission is what proves we are Jesus' disciples. "By this my Father is glorified, that you bear much fruit and so prove to be my disciples."[15]

This is the God we adore. He is the Creator and must be glorified.

Think About It:
Why does God's role as Creator demand we glorify Him?

---

14   **Psalm 19.1-4**
15   **John 15.8**

Hand in Hand

Holy, holy, holy, is the Lord God Almighty, who was and is and is to come!...Worthy are you, our Lord and God, to receive glory and honor and power, for you created all things, and by your will they existed and were created.[16]

If we are to walk with God the Creator, we must, like the creatures and elders above, cast down our crowns and worship Him. However, you must understand what is meant by this. I am not merely saying you must "go to church." Regrettably, because of our non-biblical language of calling our assemblies "worship services," many hear the word "worship" and automatically think of our assemblies.

Our assemblies are included in this worship, but are not the sum total of it. Rather, I am pointing out whether the church is assembling or not, we must worship God today.

Let me be even more clear. Though worship is not equivalent to our assemblies, we must not swing the pendulum, as so many are doing, to think worship is the same as obedience. Yes, I know that the English word "worship" is multi-faceted and in some of its usage can be applied to everything we ever do to obey God. However, that is not the way I am using the word.

I mean we must do very specific things that mirror the elders of **Revelation 4**. We must perform very specific actions that cast our golden crowns before God showing we are unworthy and He is all worthy. We must declare His greatness today and every day. We must not wait until Sunday.

Today, we need to pray and sing praises to our God. We need to lift Him up by our words and our actions. We need to go in our prayer closets and honor our God. However, we also need to let our worship lights shine before others so they me see our good works and glorify God themselves.[17]

Worshipping God should be part of our language. Sadly, we too often look at the folks who use words and phrases like "I'm blessed" or "praise God" or who go around singing songs of praise as if they are just showing off. Many Christians have come up with reasons why we shouldn't

---

16   **Revelation 4.8, 11**
17   **Matthew 5.16**

say or do those kinds of things. However, look at Paul and Silas in prison in **Acts 16.25**. They were praying and singing and they were doing it out loud. The prisoners could hear them and, apparently, so could the jailer.

"Is anyone among you suffering? Let him pray. Is anyone among you cheerful? Let him sing praise."[18] James is saying worship should be part of all our lives whether things are good or bad. We must not be ashamed of our God, but confess Him before men and do so through worship.

Certainly, we must not draw attention to ourselves so anyone will think anything about us. This is all about glorifying the Creator and encouraging others to do the same. This is the God we adore. He is the Alpha and Omega, the one who Created all things out of nothing. We need to worship Him today.

Think About It:
What can you do today to worship God? When will you do it?

Praying to Our God

Dear God, You are…

Dear God, You…

Dear God, thank You…

Dear God, forgive me for…

Dear God, help me…

3

God, the Ruler

Getting Our Bearings

Be fruitful and multiply and fill the earth and subdue it and have dominion over the fish of the sea and over the birds of the heavens and over every living thing that moves on the earth...Behold, I have given you every plant yielding seed that is on the face of all the earth, and every tree with seed in its fruit. You shall have them for food...You may surely eat of every tree of the garden, but of the tree of the knowledge of good and evil you shall not eat, for in the day that you eat of it you shall surely die.[19]

Have you ever wondered why the fruit on the tree of knowledge of good and evil was so bad? Was it poisoned? Did it contain some mystical property that changed Adam and Eve? I don't think so. Actually, the only apparent difference between that tree and the others was that God said, "Don't eat from that one." God established a rule. Violating that rule changed the nature of God's relationship with Adam and Eve.

However, this begs the question. Why did God's rule matter? Adam could have told Eve she was not allowed to eat from a certain tree or vice versa and it would not have changed a thing. God says it and the violation is earth shaking. Why? Because God is the Creator. Since God is the Creator, He is also the Ruler. As our Creator, He has the right to tell the world and us how to live.

Just as God established the laws of gravity, inertia and thermodynamics, He established the laws of morality, holiness and righteousness. God told the Israelites, "Be holy, for I am holy."[20] Peter repeated that standard

---

19   **Genesis 1.28-29; 2.16-17**
20   **Leviticus 11.44, et al**

for spiritual Israel under the New Covenant saying, "As he who called you is holy, you also be holy in all your conduct, since it is written, 'You shall be holy, for I am holy.'"[21]

God is the ultimate King of our world and our lives. Paul praised God saying, "To the King of ages, immortal, invisible, the only God, be honor and glory forever and ever. Amen."[22] Remember what Paul said when talking about Jesus Christ and His kingdom in **I Corinthians 15.24-28**:

> *Then comes the end, when he delivers the kingdom to God the Father after destroying every rule and every authority and power. For he must reign until he has put all his enemies under his feet. The last enemy to be destroyed is death. For 'God has put all things in subjection under his feet.' But when it says, 'all things are put in subjection,' it is plain that he is excepted who put all things in subjection under him. When all things are subjected to him, then the Son himself will also be subjected to him who put all things in subjection under him, that God may be all in all.*

God is the king under whom all things will ultimately find subjection. As Christians, we are already subject to Him. This is the God we adore. He is the Ruler of the world both physically and spiritually.

Think About It:

What does it mean for God to be King in your life?

---

21   **I Peter 1.15-16**

22   **I Timothy 1.17**

Hand in Hand

If God is Ruler and we want to walk hand in hand with Him, we must naturally submit as the ruled. God is the King and we are the subjects. We must, very simply, do what He says.

This stems from His role as Creator. Many Christians misunderstand this. We often say we ought to obey God because He loved us enough to send His Son to die for us. Granted, the redemption He offers through Jesus is a strong motivator for us. As John said, "We love because he first loved us."[23] However, that is not the fundamental reason we must obey God. We must obey God because He is the Creator and therefore the Ruler.

The love God offers is what gives us hope when we mess up and disobey Him. However, whether God had ever offered His Son or not, we would still owe Him our allegiance and obedience.

Think about what this means on a practical level. Many people today speak of walking with God as if it is merely some kind of emotional high. No doubt, emotions and attitudes are part of our walk with Him. However, we cannot claim to walk with God unless we are doing what He says.

Does God say, "Love your enemies"?[24] Then we must love our enemies. Does God say, "What therefore God has joined together, let not man separate"?[25] Then we must not separate it. Does God say, "Be angry and do not sin; do not let the sun go down on your anger"?[26] Then we had better demonstrate our anger without sinning and we had better deal with it quickly. God is our Creator, therefore He is our Ruler. He gets to make the rules. He is the standard. Our job is to obey Him without exceptions or excuses.

Think About It:

Have any of God's rules, commands or laws given you trouble? What must you do today to obey them?

---

23   I John 4.19
24   Matthew 5.44
25   Matthew 19.6
26   Ephesians 4.26

Praying to Our God

Dear God, You are…

Dear God, You…

Dear God, thank You…

Dear God, forgive me for…

Dear God, help me…

$$\textbf{4}$$

God in Heaven

Getting Our Bearings

"And the servants of the king of Syria said to him, 'Their gods are gods of the hills, and so they were stronger than we. But let us fight against them in the plain, and surely we shall be stronger than they.'"[27]

The Syrian king's advisors could not have been more wrong. They had laid siege against Samaria and God sent Ahab out to show them who was really God. The Israelites soundly defeated the Syrians. Their best guess was they had fought Israel on Jehovah's turf. If they moved the battle to the plains, then the Syrian god would provide victory. They did not understand Jehovah God is not God of the hills or the plains; He is God of heaven.

Look at all forms of paganism, whether Roman, Greek, Egyptian, German, Syrian, etc. We find multiple lists of gods and goddesses along with descriptions of their dominions. Neptune was the Roman god of the sea, as Poseidon was for the Greeks and Aegir for the Germans. Nut was the Egyptian goddess of the sky, as Zeus was for the Greeks. Vesta was the Roman goddess of the home. Anubis was the Egyptian god of the dead. Hephaestus was the Greek god of the forge. Frigga was the Norse goddess of motherhood. The lists go on.

There were gods and goddesses for different parts of the world, whether mountains, plains or seas. There were gods and goddesses for the different stars, planets and other heavenly bodies. Each had their special domain where they were more powerful. Our God is different. Jehovah is not God of the sea or the underworld or the sky or the home, He is the God of heaven. Thus, He is God of everything.

The gods of Rome and Greece lived on Mt. Olympus. Perhaps their earthly dwelling provides one reason the Roman and Greek concept of the divine was so diluted. Their gods were nothing more than super-powered men and women who dwelt only slightly higher than they. Our God, however, does not dwell on earth. He dwells in heaven. Moses encouraged the Israelites to pray thus, "Look down from your holy habitation, from heaven and bless your people Israel."[28] The chronicler recorded, "Then the priests and the Levites arose and blessed the people, and their voice was heard, and their prayer came to his holy habitation in heaven."[29] The Bible refers to God as "God of heaven" 25 times.

When Jesus taught His disciples to pray, He drove home the importance of remembering God's dwelling place. In **Matthew 6.9**, Jesus taught His followers to pray to "our Father in heaven." In fact, throughout the Sermon on the Mount, Jesus drew attention to God's heavenly abode six times—**Matthew 5.16, 45; 6.1, 9; 7.11, 21**.

This is the God we adore. He is not the God of the hills or of the mountains. He is not the God of America or Europe. He is not the God of the earth. He is God in heaven.

Think About It:
Look at those six references to God's heavenly abode in the Sermon on the Mount. What point was Jesus making in each case?

5.16:

5.45:

6.1:

6.9:

7.11:

7.21:

---

28   **Deuteronomy 26.15**
29   **II Chronicles 30.27**

Hand in Hand

If we are going to walk hand in hand with the God of heaven, we have to remember our place. The whole purpose of recognizing God's heavenly abode is to remember God is God and we are not. He is in heaven, we are on earth. He sees and knows all, we do not. He is the master, we are the servant. He is the king, we are the subject.

When we come to God, we are not doing so as equals. We should, therefore, humble ourselves in His presence.[30] Regrettably, many are so enamored with God's grace and condescension they have forgotten God is God. The king who has been merciful to his subject is not bringing the subject up to the King's level; neither is God doing so with us. God rebuked the Israelites in **Psalm 50.21** saying, "These things you have done, and I have been silent; you thought that I was one like yourself. But now I rebuke you and lay the charge before you." God is God and we are not. We must remember that as we pray, sing, study and teach.

Read what the preacher said about God in **Ecclesiastes 5.1-2:**

> Guard your steps when you go to the house of God. To draw near to listen is better than to offer the sacrifice of fools, for they do not know that they are doing evil. Be not rash with your mouth, nor let your heart be hasty to utter a word before God, for God is in heaven and you are on earth. Therefore let your words be few.

The preacher's whole point is the care we must take because God is in heaven and we are not. We must not be rash and hasty as we approach and address our God.

Let's keep this in perspective. God does care about us.[31] I believe He cares even about the small things in our lives. Thus, this point does not mean we should only come to God when it is really important. Rather, this means we need to take care in how we approach God no matter how important it is.

I appreciate the folks who advise us to talk to God the way we do our best friend. However, I fear this advice misses the point. God is our loving benefactor. He does care. But He is not like our best friend. Our

---

30   **James 4.10**—"Humble yourselves before the Lord…"
31   **I Peter 5.7**

best friend is on earth; our God is in heaven. We can speak flippantly, irreverently and lightly with our best friend. We had better not do so with God.

We can boldly enter the presence of God because of the blood of Jesus Christ.[32] However, we must not enter His presence brazenly or brashly. We must do so with respect and reverence, remembering our place before Him. We are the creature; He is the creator. We are the subject; He is the Ruler. We are on earth; He is in heaven.

Think About It:

What comfort do we gain from knowing our God is God in heaven and is not like the pagan gods of the earth?

---

32   **Hebrews 10.19**

Praying to Our God

Dear God, You are…

Dear God, You…

Dear God, thank You…

Dear God, forgive me for…

Dear God, help me…

5

God, the Judge

Getting Our Bearings

American government is divided into three branches: Executive, Legislative and Judicial. However, God's government has but one branch and God is it. **Isaiah 33.22** says, "For the Lord is our judge; the Lord is our lawgiver; the Lord is our king; he will save us." He is Ruler, both the Legislature who enacts the rules and the Executive who executes them. He is also the Judge.

However, few people want to think of God as judge today. We want to highlight His love, mercy, compassion, forgiveness and grace. We will give a nod to His capacity as judge, but we are convinced that is just a small part of His character reserved only for those who are so evil no one could think they would be saved. We must not allow our study of God's grace and love to cause us to overlook His judgment.

Abraham called God the judge of all the earth.[33] Hannah said, "The Lord will judge the ends of the earth."[34] Asaph said, "The heavens declare his righteousness, for God himself is judge!"[35] Isaiah said, "The Lord has taken his place to contend; he stands to judge peoples."[36] There is no doubt. God is the judge.

Really, that only makes sense. Because He is the Creator, He is our Ruler. Because He is our Ruler, He is, by rights, our Judge.

---

33 **Genesis 18.25**
34 **I Samuel 2.10**
35 **Psalm 50.6**
36 **Isaiah 3.13**

This could be a very frightening prospect. The most powerful being in the universe sits as judge over finite, weak creatures. There is nothing we can do about His judgment. If we didn't like it, we could not complain or overthrow it. If He judged unrighteously, unfairly, harshly, we could do nothing about it. However, our God is not only Judge, He is a fair and righteous judge. Further, He is a merciful Judge.

Abraham recognized that in **Genesis 18.25** asking, "Shall not the Judge of all the earth do what is just?" The Israelites under Moses were glad of God's justice. In **Deuteronomy 10.17-18** Moses wrote, "For the Lord your God is God of gods and Lord of lords, the great, the mighty, and the awesome God, who is not partial and takes no bribe. He executes justice for the fatherless and the widow, and loves the sojourner, giving him food and clothing." Moses described God in **Deuteronomy 32.4** as "the Rock, his work is perfect, for all his ways are justice. A God of faithfulness and without iniquity, just and upright is he." Through Asaph in **Psalm 75.2**, God said, "At the set time that I appoint I will judge with equity."

Isn't it wonderful to know the ultimate power of the universe and beyond does not judge us capriciously? He is not fickle. He doesn't change standards. He always judges justly. Therefore we can rejoice with the men of **Psalm 58.11** saying, "Surely there is a reward for the righteous; surely there is a God who judges on earth."

This is the God we adore. The unbounded, Creator God who rules from heaven is our just and merciful judge.

Think About It:
Why are you glad that God is our judge?

Hand in Hand

Hebrews 9.27 says, "Just as it is appointed for man to die once, and after that comes judgment." Judgment is coming for us. Each day we are a step closer. We are marching on irrevocably to the time when we will either hear, "Depart, I don't know you," or "Enter in, good and faithful servant." The myriad choices we make day in and day out are deciding that verdict even as we speak.

Picture a courthouse for a moment. You are walking to it to hear judgment for or against you. The judge is walking alongside you. Which scenario would you prefer? To be walking alongside the judge, railing at him, cursing him, ignoring him, abusing him? Or to be walking to the courthouse hand in hand with judge, knowing you have a profound relationship with the one who is about to state your sentence?

That really is happening. We are walking to the judgment hall. We are either doing so hand in hand with the Judge or we are doing so in rebellion against Him. I know which scenario I prefer.

Sadly, many folks, even Christians, have determined the picture of God as Judge is a negative one. For me, it is actually quite positive. Frankly, I'm glad God is the Judge. It could be worse. You could be the judge. Or worse still, I could be the judge.

> But with me it is a very small thing that I should be judged by you or by any human court. In fact, I do not even judge myself. For I am not aware of anything against myself, but I am not thereby acquitted. It is the Lord who judges me.[37]

Walking hand in hand with God means realizing no one else is our judge. Certainly, men may do all sorts of things to us in judgment here. They may castigate us as false teachers. They may persecute us as troublemakers. They may throw us in prison as criminals. They may even execute us as menaces to society. However, they cannot affect our eternity.

As **Matthew 10.28** says, "Do not fear those who kill the body but cannot kill the soul. Rather fear him who can destroy both soul and body in hell." Let us live without fear of those who would judge us on earth. We must not allow them to mold or guide our lives. Instead, we fear our one true Judge and therefore we walk hand in hand with Him, allowing Him to guide our lives.

When we do that, we won't have to fear God's judgment and we won't fear men. We will live in freedom simply doing what God wants.

Think About It:

How do you think we can overcome the fear of men demonstrated by some of the authorities in **John 12.42-43** and just live with God as our judge?

Praying to Our God

Dear God, You are...

Dear God, You...

Dear God, thank You...

Dear God, forgive me for...

Dear God, help me...

Walking Together

What were the most important lessons you learned about God this week?

How did this week's readings help you walk closer to God?

What advice would you give others based on this week's reading to help them walk hand in hand with God?

With what issues do you need help or prayers based on this week's reading?

What boxes have people created for God? How can we overcome those?

Why should God be our ruler? What does that mean for our lives?

What does God's abode in heaven mean for our daily walk with Him?

Why are you comforted that God is the judge?

The Triune God

"And when Jesus was baptized, immediately he went up from the water, and behold, the heavens were opened to him, and he saw the Spirit of God descending like a dove and coming to rest on him; and behold, a voice from heaven said, 'This is my beloved Son, with whom I am well pleased.'"

Matthew 3.16-17

What boxes have people created for God? How can we overcome those?

Why should God be our ruler? What does that mean for our lives?

What does God's abode in heaven mean for our daily walk with Him?

Why are you comforted that God is the judge?

WEEK TWO
The Triune God

"And when Jesus was baptized, immediately he went up from the water, and behold, the heavens were opened to him, and he saw the Spirit of God descending like a dove and coming to rest on him; and behold, a voice from heaven said, 'This is my beloved Son, with whom I am well pleased.'"

Matthew 3.16-17

6

God, the Spirit

Getting Our Bearings

Jesus said to her, "Woman, believe me, the hour is coming when neither on this mountain nor in Jerusalem will you worship the Father. You worship what you do not know; we worship what we know, for salvation is from the Jews. But the hour is coming, and is now here, when the true worshipers will worship the Father in spirit and truth, for the Father is seeking such people to worship him. God is spirit, and those who worship him must worship in spirit and truth."[38]

The Samaritan woman at the well wanted to know which mountain was really supposed to be the center of worship for God, which temple really housed Jehovah God? The Samaritan one or the one in Jerusalem? Jesus' answer probably blew her mind.

We often jump immediately to worshipping in spirit and truth and miss this amazing statement about God. God is spirit. He is not flesh and blood. More importantly, He is not gold, silver, bronze, stone or wood.

The temple question really had greater roots in idolatry than in God's true theology, even from the Old Testament. Through the Old Testament, God was leading the Israelites farther and farther away from their pagan roots, progressively revealing His nature as they could understand it. There were some great reasons for which God wanted to name a city to be the center of His worship. There were some great reasons for God to allow a temple built in His honor. However, God never intended that temple to be eternal.

He had always planned to shake it out of the way:

At that time his voice shook the earth, but now he has promised, "Yet once more I will shake not only the earth but also the heavens." This phrase, "Yet once more," indicates the removal of things that are shaken—that is, things that have been made—in order that the things that cannot be shaken may remain. Therefore let us be grateful for receiving a kingdom that cannot be shaken, and thus let us offer to God acceptable worship, with reverence and awe, for our God is a consuming fire.[39]

The "house of God" had always been destined for destruction because our God is spirit. He cannot be housed by such a structure as even Solomon recognized in **I Kings 8.27**. The temple was not built because God needed a house. It was built because God's people were not yet ready to understand His full nature or worship Him the way God ultimately intended.

The Samaritans, however, with their mixed blood and mixed religion had an even more pagan view of God.[40] They built their gods by hand. Thus, their god had to be located somewhere. A house needed to be built to protect the idol they constructed. Then, if people would worship the god, they had to be at that house.

That, however, is not our God. He is not a statue. He is not a block of wood or lump of metal. He is spirit. He is not bound by the material. He is not located in one place. Ezekiel found this out when he was deported thousands of miles from Jerusalem, unable to fulfill his priestly duties in the temple. However, he came face to face with God on His real, heavenly throne while all the way in Babylon in **Ezekiel 1**.

This is the God we adore. He is unbounded, unlimited, unlocated spirit. He is not to be found in a building somewhere, He is everywhere.

Think About It:
Read **Jeremiah 10.1-16**. What are the advantages of having a God who is spirit versus a statue?

---

39   **Hebrews 12.26-29**
40   For further explanation of this read **II Kings 17.24-41**

Hand in Hand

Jesus Himself provided our key for walking hand in hand with the God who is spirit. He is seeking those who will worship Him in spirit and truth.[41]

But what does that mean? On the surface, Jesus' statement seems odd. After all, were the Jews ever allowed to worship God in error? Were they ever allowed to worship Him without spirit?

I believe **Hebrews 10.19-22** is a commentary on Jesus' statement in **John 4.23-24**:

> *Therefore, brothers, since we have confidence to enter the holy places by the blood of Jesus, by the new and living way that he opened for us through the curtain, that is, through his flesh, and since we have a great priest over the house of God, let us draw near with a true heart in full assurance of faith, with our hearts sprinkled clean from an evil conscience and our bodies washed with pure water.*

We do not draw near to God by traveling to Jerusalem. We do not have to look toward a temple to pray. Rather, we come into the presence of God by the blood of Jesus Christ. True worshipers draw near to God with a true heart in full assurance of faith in Jesus.

Our worship is no longer tied to a city or a building. It is tied to Jesus. The time has now come to worship God the Spirit by entering the spiritual temple through Jesus Christ who is the way, the truth and the life.[42] We, who have become one spirit with the Lord, can worship God anywhere and at anytime because we have become God's temple.[43] The children of Israel were able to come into the presence of God by offering sacrifices at the temple. We come into His presence because our Sacrifice has been offered once for all.

Since we can come into God's presence by the blood of Jesus, the Hebrew writer says we need to draw near to Him. We need to come to Him and worship Him. We need to hold fast the confession of our faith knowing that God will be faithful to us through Jesus. Further, we must lift each other up, helping each other draw near to God in the assurance of faith.[44]

---

41   John 4.23-24
42   John 14.6
43   I Corinthians 6.17-20
44   Hebrews 10.23-24

We also recognize we are to worship God in accord with His Word which is truth.[45] We do not get to worship however we please, we must worship the way with which God is pleased. As **Hebrews 12.28** said, we must offer acceptable worship. Worshipping God in spirit and truth does not mean having emotional fits. No doubt, worship will cause emotion. It may cause joy. It may cause grief. However, worship is not achieved based on our emotional state. Worship is achieved based on submitting to God's will and glorifying Him His way.

Finally, worshipping in spirit and in truth demonstrates worship is not about flesh. God is not flesh, He is spirit. Therefore, true worship is not about our flesh. Whether we are speaking of congregational worship, family worship or individual worship, when the activities are more about our entertainment and pleasure than honoring God, we are not worshipping in spirit and truth. Worship should be a sacrifice to God not an appeal to our desires.

If we want to walk with the God who is Spirit, we must worship Him in spirit and truth.

Think About It:

Jesus died to give us the ability to sing, pray and otherwise worship God. What does that say about our attitude and motivation to worship God?

Praying to Our God

Dear God, You are…

Dear God, You…

Dear God, thank You…

Dear God, forgive me for…

Dear God, help me…

7

God, the Trinity

Getting Our Bearings

Peter, an apostle of Jesus Christ, to those who are elect exiles of the dispersion in Pontus, Galatia, Cappadocia, Asia, and Bithynia, according to the foreknowledge of God the Father, in the sanctification of the Spirit, for obedience to Jesus Christ and for sprinkling with his blood: May grace and peace be multiplied to you.[46]

The word "trinity" is never found in the Bible. Therefore, some Christians believe we shouldn't use it. However, according to the dictionary, the word comes from the Latin "trinitas," which merely means threeness or threefold. Whether we like the word "trinity" or not, the Bible most certainly represents the threeness of God while also representing oneness.

The Bible repeatedly presents the threefold nature of God, describing, as Peter did above, Father, Son and Holy Spirit. When Jesus was baptized, we see Him in the water, the Holy Spirit descending as a dove and the voice of the Father coming from heaven.[47] In **Matthew 28.19**, we are told to make disciples by baptizing them in the name of the Father and of the Son and of the Holy Spirit. In **John 14.26**, Jesus said the Father would send the Holy Spirit in Jesus' name and **John 15.26** said Jesus will send the Holy Spirit from the Father to bear witness to the Son. **II Corinthians 13.14** says, "The grace of the Lord Jesus Christ and the love of

---

46   I Peter 1.1-2
47   Matthew 3.16-17; Mark 1.9-11; Luke 3.21-22

God and the fellowship of the Holy Spirit be with you all." **Ephesians 4.4-6** describes the unity we must have, showing we follow one Spirit, are saved by one Lord and must submit to one God and Father. We even see evidence of the threeness of God in the Old Testament. **Isaiah 48.12-16** spoke of the first and the last who laid the foundation of the earth. At first, we are tempted to assume that is the Father. However, **vs. 16** says this one has been sent by the Lord God and His Spirit.

No doubt, we easily recognize the deity of the Father,[48] so much so that when we simply say "God," we usually refer to Him. **Colossians 2.9** explains Jesus, the Son, is also fully God, saying, "For in him the whole fullness of deity dwells bodily." **John 1.1-3** also makes this clear, claiming the Word who became flesh was with God and was God. **II Peter 1.21** shows that the Holy Spirit is also divine, saying that being moved by the Holy Spirit is equivalent to speaking from God. Lying to the Holy Spirit is equated with lying to God in **Acts 5.3-4**. Finally, **Hebrews 10.15-17** says the Holy Spirit spoke of writing His covenant on the hearts of men and forgetting their sins. This quote comes from **Jeremiah 31.33-34** and is attributed to Jehovah God. Father, Son and Spirit are all deity. They are each God.

However, they are not each other. The Bible does not present Father, Son and Spirit as three representations of the same person, but rather as three distinct persons. In **John 8.17-18**, Jesus presents Himself as a distinct witness from His Father. Thus, Jesus is not the Father. In **John 14.26**, Jesus says the Father will send the Spirit to the apostles. Thus, the Spirit is not the Father. **John 16.7** said Jesus had to leave so He could send the Holy Spirit to the apostles. Thus, Jesus is not the Spirit.

Father, Son and Holy Spirit are three divine persons, equally God and yet personally distinct. Despite their threeness, the Father, Son and Spirit are perfectly one, as **John 17.21** demonstrates. That is, they are one in unity. They perfectly coincide in purpose, goal, work and authority. The pagan gods could not shed a candle on the oneness of Jehovah.

This is the God we adore. The ruling creator judge, in three persons—Father, Son and Spirit.

John 6.27

Think About It:
How does the unity of Father, Son and Holy Spirit compare to the
gods of the pagans?

Hand in Hand

Walking hand in hand with God means walking hand in hand with
Father, Son and Holy Spirit. It means recognizing each person as fully
divine. **I Peter 1.2** helps us understand how to relate to Father, Son and
Holy Spirit, walking with them.

Our relationship with the Father is one of comfort. We are elect according to His foreknowledge. **Romans 8.28ff** explains why this is such
a comfort to us. If we love God, we know that He knows it. He does not
know it because He has seen it. He knows it because He knows all even
before we act. We do not have to worry that perhaps God has missed our
love or that Satan has somehow covered it up.

This is important because sometimes we will go through amazing
hardships. There will be times when we may wonder if God can see us or
even is looking at us. However, we know we have been elected by God's
foreknowledge and nothing can separate us from Him. We need to rest
in this comfort, for, while no one can separate us from God, we can
walk away ourselves if we choose to no longer continue in His kindness.[49]
Many have done so when times got bad. They did not trust in God the
Father and His election. They thought God had turned His back on
them, so they turned their back on Him.

Peter said we are elect by the sanctification of the Spirit. Regrettably,
because of the prevailing error of Pentecostalism, we hear sanctified by
the Spirit and often automatically think of miracles. That is not the

picture of the scripture. **I Peter 1.22-25** demonstrates our sanctification comes from obedience to the truth revealed by the Spirit. According to **John 17.16-19** we are sanctified by the truth which is God's word. **II Thessalonians 2.13** says we are saved by the Spirit's sanctification through belief in the truth.

Thus, walking with the Spirit means walking by His guidebook. Scripture came by the Holy Spirit.[50] If we want to be sanctified, we have to walk according to His lead. Just as the parallel passages **Ephesians 5.18** and **Colossians 3.16** demonstrate, being filled with the Spirit is the same as allowing the Word to dwell in us. We cannot walk with the Holy Spirit apart from walking according to the Word.

I Peter 1.2 explains we were elected to obedience in Jesus. As we have seen repeatedly, walking with God is not about emotions as much as actions. Walking with God means obeying Jesus Christ. However, this brings us full circle to remembering the foreknowledge of God. Too often we fail Jesus and submit to temptation. This is when we rely on God's foreknowledge and election. According to **Romans 8.29-30**, Christianity is a growth process. We are not just like Jesus today, but if we love God, we will be. God has determined that if we love He, we will grow and become just like Jesus.

Therefore, walking hand in hand with God means trusting God's election, pursuing the Spirit's sanctification and obeying Jesus' direction.

Think About It:
To walk with God the Spirit, you have to be led by His Word. What plan do you have for reading and studying the Bible?

Praying to Our God

Dear God, You are…

Dear God, You…

Dear God, thank You…

Dear God, forgive me for…

Dear God, help me…

8

God, the Father

Getting Our Bearings

"For us there is one God, the Father, from whom are all things and for whom we exist."[51]

"There is...one God and Father of all, who is over all and through all and in all."[52]

Since we so often refer to God the Father, God the Son and God the Holy Spirit, we might be tempted to believe the designation of Father is only about His relationship to Jesus. That, however, is not true. God is our one Father.

God is our Father because we are humans, the offspring of God. Just as Jesus could trace His ancestry to Adam, the son of God, so can we.[53] God is our Father because He is the ultimate progenitor. That is, He is the source of our life. Without Him, we could not even exist. Paul pointed this out on Mars Hill saying, "'In him we live and move and have our being'; as even some of your own poets have said, 'For we are indeed his offspring.'"[54]

As Christians, we have an even greater claim to God as our Father. We are sons of God through faith in Jesus.[55] He is not only our Father physically, but also spiritually. He is the progenitor and sustainer of our spiritual life as well.

---

51   **I Corinthians 8.6**
52   **Ephesians 4.4, 6**
53   Luke 3.38
54   **Acts 17.28**
55   **Galatians 3.26**

Isaiah 64.8 says, "But now, O Lord, you are our Father; we are the clay, and you are our potter; we are all the work of your hand." God is our Father because we have given Him authority in our lives to mold us into His image and the image of His Son.[56] **Ephesians 2.10** says, "We are his workmanship, created in Christ Jesus for good works, which God prepared beforehand, that we should walk in them."

In **Mark 14.36**, Jesus cried out to the Father using a very special term saying, "Abba, Father." Lest we think this was reserved for the special relationship between Jesus and the Father, **Romans 8.15** and **Galatians 4.6** both say we are given the spirit of adoption by which we may also cry out "Abba! Father!"

Sadly, many today have read our own modern culture back into these passages and made the dreadful suggestion that we pray to God calling Him, "Daddy." There is no doubt we have a very special and loving relationship with our Father in heaven, however, we need to recognize the absolute respect and reverence for fathers in the Biblical culture that is not expressed by our endearing term of "Daddy."

Having said that, we must admit that the Aramaic term Abba was such a special term because it was, in fact, the word an infant could form first. Thus, this phrase does represent the absolute dependence of a child crying out to his or her father. We can come to God as little children who can do nothing but turn to their Father to protect them, fix their problems, kiss their hurts and comfort their sorrows.

However, the very special place of this term is demonstrated in the two passages in which we are told we can use it (**Romans 8.15** and **Galatians 4.6**). In both passages, the contrast is made between being a slave and being a son. Though slaves might address their master as father, they were never allowed to use this special term reserved for actual children. Our ability to cry out "Abba! Father!" shows we have not been given a spirit of slavery to God, but a spirit of adoption. That is, we do not submit to God because He is cracking the whip of mastery, but because He is leading us in the love of a Father. What a wonderful relationship we have with Him.

This is the God we adore. Though He is the ruler of the universe, He is our loving Father to whom we can turn as little children who need the protecting arm of a Father.

Think About It:
What comfort do you receive from knowing God is our Father?

👋 Hand in Hand

If we are going to walk hand in hand with God our Abba, Father, we need to keep our hand in His. Look more closely at the contexts of **Romans 8.15** and **Galatians 4.6**.

> So then brothers, we are debtors, not to the flesh to live according to the flesh. For if you live according to the flesh you will die, but if by the Spirit you put to death the deeds of the body, you will live. For all who are led by the Spirit of God are sons of God. For you did not receive the spirit of slavery to fall back into fear, but have received the Spirit of adoption as sons, by whom we cry, "Abba! Father!" The Spirit himself bears witness with our spirit that we are children of God, and if children, then heirs—heirs of God and fellow heirs with Christ, provided we suffer with him in order that we may also be glorified with him.[57]

> And because you are sons, God has sent the Spirit of his Son into our hearts, crying, "Abba! Father!" So you are no longer a slave, but a son, and if a son, then an heir through God. Formerly, when you did not know God, you were enslaved to those that by nature are not gods. But now that you have come to know God, or rather to be known by God, how can you turn back again to the weak and worthless elementary principles of the world, whose slave you want to be once more?[58]

In both passages, the problem was the Christians were letting go of the Father's hand and turning back to their old walk. There is a reason our Father wants us to hold His hand. I don't know how many times I have been walking with my children through a parking lot or on a road and had to remind them over and again to hold my hand. Holding my hand

---

57   **Romans 8.12-17**
58   **Galatians 4.6-9**

is for their protection. The drivers in the cars can't see them like they can me. My children don't know how to pay attention like I do. Sometimes however, they want to let go so they can go splash in a puddle, walk on a curb or just run around. I have to call them back each time and explain, "Don't let go of my hand. It's for your own good."

Walking hand in hand with God is for our own good. There may be times when we want to spread our wings and do our own thing. There may be times when our old ways are calling us and appear more inviting. However, we hold God's hand for our protection and safety. Satan doesn't fear us, but he fears God. We need God walking with us if we will overcome Satan.

Therefore, if we want to walk hand in hand with God, we need to keep our hand in His no matter what Satan displays off in the distance to get us to walk away.

Think About it:
Considering all we have learned about God already, how do you think we can keep our hand in God's every day?

Praying to Our God

Dear God, You are…

Dear God, You…

Dear God, thank You…

Dear God, forgive me for…

Dear God, help me…

(**9**)

God, the Son

Getting Our Bearings

> *Long ago, at many times and in many ways, God spoke to our fa-*
> *thers by the prophets, but in these last days he has spoken to us by his Son,*
> *whom he appointed the heir of all things, through whom also he created*
> *the world. He is the radiance of the glory of God and the exact imprint*
> *of his nature, and he upholds the universe by the word of his power.*
> *After making purification for sins, he sat down at the right hand of the*
> *Majesty on high, having become as much superior to angels as the name*
> *he has inherited is more excellent than theirs.*[59]

> *In the beginning was the Word, and the Word was with God, and the*
> *Word was God…And the Word became flesh and dwelt among us, and*
> *we have seen his glory, glory as of the only Son from the Father, full of*
> *grace and truth…No one has ever seen God; the only God, who is at the*
> *Father's side, he has made him known.*[60]

We most commonly view Jesus as God the Son because He was begotten into the world through Mary by the power of the Holy Spirit. Certainly that is true and He is the Son of God in that sense. However, His sonship preceded His incarnation. He is God the Son not merely because of His birth into the world but because of His submission to the Father's will.

Though Jesus was in the form of God, equal with the Father in divinity, He voluntarily submitted as a Son to the Father's plan. He left the abode of heaven and came into the world as a man. He is not the Son

---

59   **Hebrews 1.1-4**
60   **John 1.1, 14, 18**

because of His birth. He is the Son because of His submission. That is
why Paul quoted **Psalm 2.7**[61] to refer to Jesus' resurrection, not His birth
in **Acts 13.33**. Paul also wrote in **Romans 1.4** that Jesus was "declared
to be the Son of God in power according to the Spirit of holiness by his
resurrection from the dead."

Jesus, who was fully God, that is, fully divine,[62] is the Son because of
His submission and obedience. However, make note of the very interest-
ing statement in **Hebrews 5.8**: "Although he was a son, he learned obedience through what he suffered." No doubt, Jesus knew what obedience
was before His suffering. The point is continued obedience throughout
suffering created an experiential knowledge that perfected Him through
submission, making Him the source of our salvation.[63] In other words,
obedience and submission are not really obedience and submission until
they endure under duress. Jesus was perfected as God the Son because
He continued His submission even through suffering.

Finally, the great importance of God the Son is seen in **John 1.18**,
"No one has ever seen God; the only God, who is at the Father's side, he
has made him known," and **John 14.9**, "Have I been with you so long,
and you still do not know me, Philip? Whoever has seen me has seen the
Father."

The Son made the Father known. The Son is the image of the Father.
If we want to know God, we must know the Son of God. No wonder
there is no way to get to the Father, but through the Son.[64] We can't even
know the Father unless we know the Son.

This is the God we adore. Though our creator, He is willing to voluntarily submit Himself in obedience to a plan that will save us. Through
this, He served not only the Father, but He has served the children as
well.

---

61 "The Lord said to me, 'You are my Son, today I have begotten you.'"
62 **Colossians 2.9**—"For in him the whole fullness of deity dwells bodily."
63 **Hebrews 5.9**
64 **John 14.6**—"I am the way, and the truth, and the life. No one comes to the Father
except through me."

Think About It:
What does Jesus' life tell you about God?

Hand in Hand

In **Luke 10.38-42**, Martha encouraged Jesus to rebuke Mary for sitting at His feet while the duties of hostess were left wanting. But Jesus responded, "Martha, Martha, you are anxious and troubled about many things, but one thing is necessary." Paul demonstrated that one thing in **Philippians 3.8** saying, "Indeed, I count everything as loss because of the surpassing worth of knowing Christ Jesus my Lord."

There are many fun things in this life. There are many good things in this life. There are many meaningful things in this life. However, there is only one necessary thing in this life—knowing Jesus, God the Son. By knowing the Son, we know the Father. By knowing the Son, we gain eternal life.[65] By knowing the Son, we walk with God.

Galatians 2.20 defines walking with the Son. "I have been crucified with Christ. It is no longer I who live, but Christ who lives in me. And the life I now live in the flesh I live by faith in the Son of God, who loved me and gave himself for me." Once again we learn walking with God does not mean having an emotional fit at the mention of His name. Knowing Jesus, walking with Jesus means believing what He has said and taught and living it. It means letting our lives be governed by what Jesus wants, not what we want.

There is only one way to know what Jesus taught and how Jesus lived. There is only one way for us to know Jesus. That way is not through the feelings of our heart. That way is not to follow what we are sure Jesus would want based on how we feel. That way is to open the Word of God and see what is revealed about Jesus within its pages. John explained that he was declaring the Son to us in his writings so we might know Him and have fellowship with Him.[66]

---

65   I John 5.11-12
66   I John 1.1-4

However, we need to understand that our relationship with the Son and, therefore, the Father, will not always be like strolling down the rose-lined garden path. The Son learned obedience through suffering and if we walk with Him, we will walk that path as well. **Romans 8.16-17** says, "The Spirit himself bears witness with our spirit that we are children of God, and if children, then heirs—heirs of God and fellow heirs with Christ, provided we suffer with him in order that we may also be glorified with him."

We are heirs with Christ when we suffer with Christ. Regrettably, many today believe they are abandoned by God when they suffer. The fact is, we are most like Jesus when we suffer. We are closest to Him when we suffer, especially if we suffer for His cause.

Paul said "through many tribulations we must enter the kingdom of God."[67] If we want to walk with God, we must be prepared for obstacles in our path. We must be prepared to suffer. However, we can take comfort because we have a high priest who has come through the heavens to live as one of us, suffer as one of us and therefore can help us in our suffering.[68]

May we learn obedience as He did, walking with Him, suffering with Him and coming out on the other side perfected by His grace through our suffering.

Think About It:

How does suffering with Jesus make us complete and perfect?

---

67   **Acts 14.22**
68   **Hebrews 2.14-18**

Praying to Our God

Dear God, You are…

Dear God, You…

Dear God, thank You…

Dear God, forgive me for…

Dear God, help me…

⑩

God, the Holy Spirit

✴ Getting Our Bearings

Nevertheless, I tell you the truth: it is to your advantage that I go away, for if I do not go away, the Helper will not come to you. But if I go, I will send him to you. And when he comes, he will convict the world concerning sin and righteousness and judgment: concerning sin, because they do not believe in me; concerning righteousness, because I go to the Father, and you will see me no longer; concerning judgment, because the ruler of the world is judged. I still have many things to say to you, but you cannot bear them now. When the Spirit of truth comes, he will guide you into all the truth, for he will not speak on his own authority, but whatever he hears he will speak, and he will declare to you the things that are to come. He will glorify me, for he will take what is mine and declare it to you. All that the Father has is mine; therefore I said that he will take what is mine and declare it to you.[69]

According to God the Son, God the Holy Spirit had a fourfold job. The Holy Spirit would guide the apostles into all truth, but would also convict the world concerning sin, righteousness and judgment.

The Holy Spirit is the Helper. He is our helper. But Jesus does not present this help as some kind of ushy-mushy ethereal hand-holding. It is not some kind of unseen shoulder on which to cry. The Holy Spirit helps by guiding us into truth. The truth is exactly what Jesus wants us to know because the Holy Spirit does not make up truth or speak on His own authority, but speaks what the Son wants us to hear. The Holy Spirit takes what is Jesus' and proclaims that to us.

Beyond that, the main work of the Holy Spirit is conviction in three areas—sin, righteousness and judgment. The Spirit convicts the world of sin, Jesus said, because the world did not believe in Him. This ties back to **John 1.9-11**. Jesus came into the world. He came unto His own. But they did not receive Him. Jesus had shown the light. He had exposed sin, but His own people rejected Him. Yet, He would give them another opportunity. The Holy Spirit would come.

Through the miraculous gifts given to God's children, the Holy Spirit exposed the works of the flesh. When the miraculous gifts were no longer needed, the Holy Spirit had produced the Scriptures that were profitable to reprove and correct.[70] The world can be convicted of sin if they will merely pick up the Bible and read it.

The Holy Spirit would convict the world of righteousness because Jesus was going to the Father and we can no longer see Him. Jesus was righteousness incarnate. If we see His life, we see righteousness. However, He is no longer here. Thus the Holy Spirit was sent to help by lighting a lamp along the path of righteousness.

Again, by the miraculous gifts He bestowed upon His servants, the Holy Spirit lit the way of the Fruit of the Spirit. When the miraculous gifts were no longer necessary, the Spirit had left behind the Scriptures which train us in all righteousness.[71] The world can know righteousness if it will merely pick up the Bible and read it.

The Holy Spirit would convict the world concerning judgment because the ruler of this world is judged. Jesus reminds us of what He had said in **John 12.31-33**: "'Now is the judgment of this world; now will the ruler of this world be cast out. And I, when I am lifted up from the earth, will draw all people to myself.' He said this to show by what kind of death he was going to die." The point is that in Jesus' crucifixion, the great enemy, the ruler of the world, Satan, had been judged. He had lost.

This reminds me of a game Marita and I play called Pente. The point is to either place 5 stones in a row or capture 10 of your opponent's stones. Usually before the game is actually ended, there comes a point at which we both know who will win. One of us has a position on the board that cannot be stopped. However, we always play it to the bitter end to see exactly how it pans out. That is what Satan is going through.

---

70   II Timothy 3.16-17
71   Ibid.

He has already lost. He is now simply trying to see how many playing pieces he can capture before it is finally over.

The Holy Spirit is convicting the world of judgment because judgment is certain. We may not see it as such because we look with human eyes. However, if we believe the Bible's story, we know it is too late for those who side with the enemy. No matter how much victory they think they are gaining, they will lose in the end. The game is already up. God has already won. The Holy Spirit is working to convict the world of this so more souls will be saved from the judgment to come.

Remember, the Holy Spirit only speaks the words of Jesus. In **John 12.48,** Jesus promised that the word He speaks will judge us. If we wish to avoid the judgment, we had best follow the word of Jesus revealed by the Spirit.

This is the God we adore. Sovereign ruler of the universe, creator of mankind whose Holy Spirit works to convict us that we might turn from sin, pursue righteousness and be prepared for the coming judgment, having followed His word into all truth.

Think About It:
Read **II Timothy 3.16-17,** what is the role of the Bible in the Holy Spirit's work today?

🖐 Hand in Hand

"But I say, walk by the Spirit, and you will not gratify the desires of the flesh."[72]

If we are going to walk hand in hand with God, we must follow the lead of the Spirit. The Spirit, through the Word, is lighting the way for us. We must pursue His way. That means turning our back on the passions of our flesh.

Paul said we all once walked according to the passions of our flesh, carrying out the desires of the body and the mind.[73] Now we must turn our backs on those desires because they are against the Spirit.[74] The fruit of the Spirit is love, joy, peace, patience, kindness, goodness, faithfulness, gentleness and self control.[75] The works of the flesh, however, are sexual immorality, impurity, sensuality, idolatry, sorcery, enmity, strife, jealousy, fits of anger, rivalries, dissensions, divisions, envy, drunkenness, orgies and things like these.[76]

If we would walk hand in hand with God, we must ask ourselves, "Am I pursuing the works of the flesh or the fruit of the Spirit?" Does the party I am attending fall more in line with joy and goodness or drunkenness and orgies? Do the clothes I am wearing fall more in line with goodness and self-control or impurity and sensuality? Do the friends I hang out with promote love, joy and peace or enmity, strife and jealousy? Does my daily path promote faithfulness and love or immorality and idolatry?

"Those who belong to Christ Jesus have crucified the flesh with its passions and desires. If we live by the Spirit, let us also walk by the Spirit."[77]

Of course, we cannot walk by the Spirit without being in the Word. As **II Peter 1.20-21** explains, the Scriptures we hold in our hand are the work of the Holy Spirit. Even were the Holy Spirit working in some kind of personally miraculous way, we could only know the influence we felt was from Him if it lined up with the Bible.

72	Galatians 5.16
73	Ephesians 2.3
74	Galatians 5.17
75	Galatians 5.22-23
76	Galatians 5.19-21
77	Galatians 5.24-25

We must spend time in the word every day. Then our way can be lit. As David wrote, "Your word is a lamp to my feet and a light to my path."[78] If we wish to be shepherded in the paths of righteousness, we must follow the Spirit's lead through the Spirit's word.

Think About It:

Which part of the fruit of the Spirit do you do the best at? …the worst?

What can you do this week to take both of these aspects of your spiritual life up to a new level?

Praying to Our God

Dear God, You are…

Dear God, You…

Dear God, thank You…

Dear God, forgive me for…

Dear God, help me…

Walking Together

What were the most important lessons you learned about God this week?

How did this week's readings help you walk closer to God?

What advice would you give others based on this week's reading to help them walk hand in hand with God?

With what issues do you need help or prayers based on this week's reading?

How does knowing God is Spirit impact your worship?

What comfort does God's fatherhood bring you in your daily walk with Him?

Since Jesus displays the Father, what does the life of Jesus tell you about God in general?

What advice would you give others to help them avoid the works of the flesh and pursue the fruit of the Spirit?

Week Three
God On Earth

"In the beginning was the Word, and the Word was with God, and the Word was God. He was in the beginning with God. All things were made through him, and without him was not anything made that was made…And the Word became flesh and dwelt among us, and we have seen his glory, glory as of the only Son from the Father, full of grace and truth."

John 1.1-3, 14

11

God, the Incarnation

Getting Our Bearings

Since therefore the children share in flesh and blood, he himself likewise partook of the same things, that through death he might destroy the one who has the power of death, that is, the devil, and deliver all those who through fear of death were subject to lifelong slavery. For surely it is not angels that he helps, but he helps the offspring of Abraham. Therefore he had to be made like his brothers in every respect, so that he might become a merciful and faithful high priest in the service of God, to make propitiation for the sins of the people. For because he himself has suffered when tempted, he is able to help those who are being tempted.[79]

God, by Himself, is almost impossible to fathom. The infinity of the divine sends our heads spinning. However, take that infinity and put it in human form and you have the all-time greatest mystery of the gospel message. **John 1.14** says the Word, which is God, became flesh and dwelt among us.

Let us lay aside any delusions that we can fully understand what happened here. Let us lay aside the arguments and debates that pretend to know exactly how deity and humanity intersected. We must simply accept what the Scriptures say. Jesus on earth was God, fully divine.[80] Yet He was also a man, fully human.[81] Jesus was not God who looked like a man. This is not a repeat of what happened in **Genesis 18**, in which God appeared as a man. This was a unique occurrence in history. God did not appear as man, He became man.

---

79   **Hebrews 2.14-18**
80   **John 1.1-18; Colossians 2.9**
81   **I Timothy 2.5**

I have always liked the way J.I. Packer described the incarnation:

The Word had become flesh: a real human baby. He had not ceased to be God; he was no less God then than before; but he had begun to be man. He was not now God minus some elements of his deity, but God plus all that he had made his own by taking manhood to himself. He who made man was now learning what it felt like to be man.[82]

One misnomer needs to be corrected. I don't know how many times I have discussed Jesus' prayer in **Matthew 26.39** and heard someone say, "This prayer shows Jesus' human side." I have yet to find any passage in scripture that says Jesus had a human side and a divine side. He was not dualistic, sometimes acting as deity and sometimes acting as human. Jesus was what He was—God in the flesh. He was all human and all God all at the same time. We do not see Jesus' human side or humanity acting in this passage. We see Jesus as He was—both human and divine.

What is most amazing about this incarnation is the why question. Why did God become flesh? God could have saved mankind however He wanted. He is God. He created the world and He established the rules. However, His plan said the Word must become flesh and dwell among us.

Hebrews 2.14-18 said it was so Jesus could be our merciful and faithful high priest. Having suffered as a human, He is now able to help us who are human. Yet, isn't He God? Doesn't He know all? Is He like a man, having to experience something to truly know it? Of course not. Therefore, when we get to the bottom of it, God did not become man because He needed to. He did so for our benefit. He could help us without becoming human, but how much more confidence do we have because He did. When we face troubles, He comes to us with help because He has "been there, done that."

What amazing love. What amazing mercy. What an amazing God. This is the God we adore, the sovereign creator and ruler of the universe who became one of us so we might have confidence in His help.

Think About It:

What comfort do you gain as you think about God coming in the flesh?

---

82   *Knowing God*, Intervarsity Press, Downers Grove, IL, 1973p 57.

Hand in Hand

Since then we have a great high priest who has passed through the heavens, Jesus, the Son of God, let us hold fast our confession. For we do not have a high priest who is unable to sympathize with our weaknesses, but one who in every respect has been tempted as we are, yet without sin. Let us then with confidence draw near to the throne of grace, that we may receive mercy and find grace to help in time of need.[83]

If we are going to walk hand in hand with God, we must learn the great lesson of the incarnation. Jesus dwelt among us that we might have confidence in His ability to help us. We, therefore, need to turn to him for help and grace in our time of need.

Sadly, we spend most of our time acting as though we don't really have times of need. Certainly, we all talk about those times when there is nothing we can do but pray. Yet, we often treat that like a last resort. Prayer and leaning on God must be our first resort.

We must devote every day to God, asking for His strength to face and overcome whatever Satan will hurl at us. Paul demonstrated this in **II Corinthians 12.7-10**. He prayed repeatedly for God to remove his thorn in the flesh. Yet, God refused, claiming His grace was enough. Note what Paul learned from the experience:

Therefore I will boast all the more gladly of my weaknesses, so that the power of Christ may rest upon me. For the sake of Christ, then, I am content with weaknesses, insults, hardships, persecutions, and calamities. For when I am weak, then I am strong.

We must quit thinking we are so strong and only need God to give us the final nudge. We must learn to boast in our weaknesses. Only when we realize how truly weak we are can we become a vessel for God's strength. Think about Moses. When he thought he was someone who could deliver God's people, he fled Egypt, fearing for his life because even his own people rejected him. However, when he cowered before the burning bush proclaiming how weak and unqualified he was to do the job, then God was able to deliver Israel through him.

---

83   **Hebrews 4.14-16**

Let us recognize that we cannot overcome the devil today on our own strength. We cannot obey the Lord from our own strength. Let us begin the day casting ourselves on God's mercy, praying, studying His word and simply doing what He said, trusting Him for the strength to continue on. Only then can we walk hand in hand with God.

As we face this terrifying prospect of fighting against the enemy today, let us remember that the one who gives us strength has been there. He has done it. He overcame. He can overcome through us again.

Think About It:

What must you do today if you are going to merely rely on God for your strength?

Praying to Our God

Dear God, You are...

Dear God, You...

Dear God, thank You...

Dear God, forgive me for...

Dear God, help me...

12

God, the Servant

Getting Our Bearings

It shall not be so among you. But whoever would be great among you must be your servant, and whoever would be first among you must be your slave, even as the Son of Man came not to be served but to serve, and to give his life a ransom for many.[84]

This is perhaps the reason the Greeks viewed the Gospel as folly.[85] Gods were to be served; they were not to be servants. As intimated in the last chapter, the incarnation was, in fact, the greatest act of service. The incarnation was not for God. It was for us.

Jesus willingly gave of Himself in order to lift us up. He put our interests above His own. He considered us as more significant than Himself. Paul stated this in **Philippians 2.3-5**, explaining we should have the same mind. He went on to say Jesus "made himself nothing, taking the form of a servant, being born in the likeness of men."[86] How amazing is that? Jesus, the one who is truly worthy,[87] lifted us up as worthy of service.

Perhaps one of the most profound displays of Jesus, God the Servant, is found in **John 13**. In the midst of the Passover feast with the disciples, Jesus stood up, girt himself with a towel and washed His disciples' feet. This task was the lowliest and meanest of duties given to slaves. A master shouldn't do this. Yet Jesus turned the social order upside down.

---

84   Matthew 20.26-28
85   I Corinthians 1.23
86   Philippians 2.7
87   Revelation 5.12-13

We have no way of knowing the order of the apostles around that table. Perhaps Peter was the first and the other apostles learned from him to keep their mouths shut. Perhaps he watched with shocked indignation as the other apostles said nothing while Jesus played the servant. In either case, Peter would not have it. There was no way. Jesus was the Master; He was not the servant. Jesus would not wash his feet. It was almost as if Peter thought this was a test and he knew how to pass. He refused to let Jesus wash his feet. However, all he had done was demonstrate he didn't understand the God who was before him. Jesus, though divine, is indeed a servant.

Yet, Jesus did not stop by washing His disciples' feet. He then took them across the brook Kidron and into the Garden of Gethsemane where He was arrested. He was carried through mock trials and then nailed to a cross. He did not wash our feet; He washed our souls with His blood. What service.

This is the God we adore. Though divine and so far above us we cannot even fathom His greatness, He condescends to serve us. How humbling.

Think About It:

What surprises you about Jesus' actions in **John 13?**

Hand in Hand

"Do you understand what I have done to you? You call me Teacher and Lord, and you are right, for so I am. If I then, your Lord and Teacher, have washed your feet, you also ought to wash one another's feet. For I have given you an example, that you also should do just as I have done to you."[88]

Does this statement surprise you? It surprises me. I expect Jesus to say, "If I then wash your feet, how much more ought you to wash Mine?" Yet He doesn't. He didn't take this opportunity to say we ought to serve Him. Rather, He took this opportunity to say we ought to serve one another.

"What?!" we cry. "Wash his feet? Wash her feet? Surely you are joking, Jesus. I have my standards. There are just some things I don't do and washing feet is one." Yes, I know this story is not telling us we must actually wash feet, but it is teaching us to serve others even when it means performing low and menial acts. How easy it is for us to believe some things are beneath our dignity. Surely God did not expect us to do those. However, Jesus did it. We may have a hard time understanding this, but washing someone else's feet was about as lowly and menial a task anyone could perform in Jesus' day, but He did it anyway.

Regrettably, many Christians want to have a wonderful walk with Jesus, holding His hand as we walk through the rose garden of life. As they walk, they wish they did not have to be bothered with all those fellow travelers. If everyone else could just leave them alone, their walk with Jesus would be peaceful and serene.

However, we actually cannot walk hand in hand with God unless we are also walking hand in hand with God's other children. In fact, we cannot walk hand in hand with God unless we are helping carry God's other children. **Galatians 6.1** exhorts us to "Bear one another's burdens, and so fulfill the law of Christ."

Jesus has called us to be servants like Him. Sadly, so few actually want to serve today. No doubt, we don't mind serving if it doesn't get in the way of our schedule or ask us to do something we don't like. We will serve as long as it doesn't cost us anything. Service, however, is a sacrifice.

Look at how much Jesus willingly gave in order to serve us. How much more ought we be willing to give in order to serve one another? So what if it makes us miss our favorite tv show. So what if it takes us all day. So what if it means getting out our grubby clothes and acting like one of "those people." So what.

Jesus left the realm of heaven to live as one of us. He did so to serve us. Let us walk with Him by serving His brethren.

Think About It:
Who will you serve this week?

What will you do for them?

Praying to Our God

Dear God, You are…

Dear God, You…

Dear God, thank You…

Dear God, forgive me for…

Dear God, help me…

13

God, the Sacrifice

Getting Our Bearings

"The next day he saw Jesus coming toward him, and said, 'Behold, the Lamb of God, who takes away the sin of the world!'"[89]

God created us to glorify Him through our fellowship with Him. As we have learned already, He is our standard of holiness. However, we have fallen short of that standard.[90] We have sinned and, therefore, been separated from God.[91] The fellowship for which God created us has been destroyed of our own doing.

Our sin has declared a penalty. **Romans 6.23** says, "The wages of sin is death." **Ezekiel 18.20** says, "The soul who sins shall die." Death is the penalty for sin. We are all under that penalty, and, left to ourselves, there is no hope for us.

However, the just God, who is judge, does not merely want to enact judgment on us because of our sins. In **Ezekiel 18.23**, God continued by saying, "Have I any pleasure in the death of the wicked, declares the Lord God, and not rather that he should turn from his way and live?" Then again in **Ezekiel 33.11**, "As I live, declares the Lord God, I have no pleasure in the death of the wicked, but that the wicked turn from his way and live; turn back, turn back from your evil ways, for why will you die?"

---

89   **John 1.29**
90   **Romans 3.10-18, 23**
91   **Isaiah 59.1-2**

The just God doesn't want to condemn us, but to save us. Therefore He came up with a plan that would allow for His justice as well as His mercy. That plan was sacrifice. **Leviticus 16** describes the sacrifices on the Day of Atonement. On that day, two goats were offered. Upon one, the priest figuratively placed the sins of the people and then sent it off into the wilderness. The other was slain. Notice what happened here. The sins of the people were attributed to the goat and taken away. The death of the goat was attributed to the people and they lived. God said this worked because "the life of the flesh is in the blood, and I have given it for you on the altar to make atonement for your souls, for it is the blood that makes atonement by the life."[92] The life is in the blood. The sacrifice's shed blood is the death attributed to the sinner that makes atonement.

Sacrifice was the mainstay of the Old Testament religion. They had sacrifices every day, extra sacrifices on the Sabbath, even more sacrifices at the beginning of months and even more on special days. According to **Numbers 28-29** there were 1251 mandatory sacrifices per year, not counting the free will and sin sacrifices the people offered every day. Can you just imagine what the Temple was like? No doubt it reeked of death's stench. Can you envision the blood, the flies, the priests covered like butchers in the filth of slaughter?

For hundreds of years the Jews traveled to Jerusalem, pilgrimaged to the Temple to learn the lesson of sacrifice. Can you imagine having grown up under that system? Can you imagine having taken your own unblemished lambs to the Temple and watched their blood spilt so you wouldn't have to die for your sins? Then one day, as you walk with John, who has been baptizing people telling them to look for the Messiah, he stops with a gasp, points at a man you know to be his cousin and says, "Behold, the Lamb of God, who takes away the sins of the world."[93]

Jesus did not come into the world to sit on Herod's throne. He did not come into the world to sit on Caesar's throne. He came into the world to die, but not just any death. He came into the world to die as a sacrifice so you didn't have to. He bore your sins on the cross and His death is attributed to you.

---

92   **Leviticus 17.11**
93   **John 1.29, 36**

II Corinthians 5.14-15 says, "...we have concluded this: that one has died for all, therefore all have died; and he died for all, that those who live might no longer live for themselves but for him who for their sake died and was raised." Jesus died; through Him, we have all died. His death was attributed to us and our sins were laid on Him.[94]

This is the God we adore. Though He is the sovereign ruler and judge of all mankind, He wanted to save mankind. Therefore, He entered the world to be the propitiating sacrifice that would save us from ourselves.

Think About It:
What do you learn about Jesus' sacrifice from **Isaiah 53**?

Hand in Hand

Do you not know that all of us who have been baptized into Christ Jesus were baptized into his death? We were buried therefore with him by baptism into death, in order that, just as Christ was raised from the dead by the glory of the Father, we too might walk in newness of life. For if we have been united with him in a death like his, we shall certainly be united with him in a resurrection like his. We know that our old self was crucified with him in order that the body of sin might be brought to nothing, so that we would no longer be enslaved to sin. For one who has died has been set free from sins. Now if we have died with Christ, we believe that we will also live with him.[95]

If we want to walk hand in hand with God, the Sacrifice, we must be sacrificed with Him. That is, we must be crucified with Him. That crucifixion does not happen the moment we believe in Jesus. We can believe in Jesus for years and never be crucified with him. That crucifixion takes place when we finally believe Jesus and submit to Him in baptism, buried with Him that we might be raised with Him to walk in newness of life.

---

94   **I Peter 2.24**
95   **Romans 6.3-8**

We are not crucified with Christ through mere intellectual assent. We are not crucified with Christ through prayer. We are not crucified with Christ through trying to reform our lives. We are not crucified with Christ by "going to church." We are crucified with Christ when we are baptized in His name for the remission of sins. Then, through faith, we are raised by the powerful working of God.[96] We are made a new creation, the old things have been put away and all things have become new for us.[97]

However, we must not think it stops there. Now that we are a new creation by God's workmanship, we are to walk in the good works for which God has created us. "For we are his workmanship, created in Christ Jesus for good works, which God prepared beforehand, that we should walk in them."[98]

We sacrifice ourselves with Christ on His cross when we submit to baptism. Then we continue to be a sacrifice with Jesus. "Present your bodies as a living sacrifice, holy and acceptable to God, which is your spiritual worship."[99] Sadly, because of our necessary debates about the work of the church and the authority of the Bible regarding the local congregation, it seems that many Christians have lost sight of the fact that Jesus saves us as individuals, not congregations. Christianity is first and foremost about our individual lives and only secondarily about our lives together in the collective. As someone has said, "The trouble with a living sacrifice is it keeps crawling off the altar." We must stay on the altar after our crucifixion with Jesus.

Before we spend our time making sure our congregations are working correctly, we must make sure we are working correctly as individual Christians. We must sacrifice ourselves on Jesus' altar. Our lives must be about serving Him no matter the cost, walking with Him in His works, not our own.

Think About It:

What works do we need to do to walk hand in hand with God as His workmanship?

96	Colossians 2.12
97	II Corinthians 5.17
98	Ephesians 2.10
99	Romans 12.1

Praying to Our God

Dear God, You are…

Dear God, You…

Dear God, thank You…

Dear God, forgive me for…

Dear God, help me…

14

God, the Savior

Getting Our Bearings

"Fear not, for behold, I bring you good news of great joy that will be for all the people. For unto you is born this day in the city of David a Savior, who is Christ the Lord."[100]

"Today salvation has come to this house, since he also is a son of Abraham. For the Son of Man came to seek and to save the lost."[101]

"Accept Jesus as your personal savior." This language is so common, I'm not sure we fully appreciate what this means. God is our Savior. We sing, "I was lost, but now I'm found." However, do we appreciate that? Regrettably, far too many Christians, especially those who were raised by Christians or by religious parents, often view this as merely an academic issue.

We can have too good a view of ourselves before we submitted to God in baptism. Too often we can think, "I was never so bad. Yes, I was lost, but mostly I obeyed God." However, if God is our Savior, that means we needed saving.

The person in the life boat does not need saving. The person swimming in the water does not need saving. Only the person flailing about sinking under the water needs saving. That is exactly who we were. Paul said:

And you were dead in the trespasses and sins in which you once walked, following the course of this world...among whom we all once lived in the passions of our flesh, carrying out the desires of the body and the mind, and were by nature

children of wrath, like the rest of mankind. But God, being rich in mercy...
made us alive together with Christ—by grace you have been saved...[102]

We were enslaved by sin. We were on a one way course to hell and
eternal torment. We could do nothing about it. Then God sent His Son
and plucked us from the fire. Like Israel passing through the Red Sea,
Daniel surviving the lions' den and Hananiah, Meshael and Azariah
enduring the fiery furnace, we overcame the captivity of sin and Satan.

However, we must recognize the point God made to His children
over and over again. In **Isaiah 43.11**, He said, "I, I am the Lord, and
besides me there is no savior." Again in **Isaiah 45.21**, "And there is no
other god besides me, a righteous God and Savior; there is none besides
me." Then in **Hosea 13.4**, "I am the Lord your God from the land of
Egypt; you know no God but me, and besides me there is no savior."

We did not save ourselves by our baptism. The preacher did not save
us by his teaching. The church did not save us by its work. God saved us
by His gracious hand.

Finally, understand what salvation is. "Salvation" was not merely a
spiritual term. It might also refer to freeing from captivity. It could
refer to healing. It meant to liberate and make whole. God is our liberator. God is our healer. God is our preserver. Only God can set us free
from the spiritual chains that bind us. Even as growing Christians we
are sometimes overcome. Depression, anxiety, guilt, fear attack us from
all around. Satan will try to offer us saviors. Money, alcohol, drugs, sex,
even pain is offered by Satan to be our saviors. These, however, offer
nothing but further enslavement. Only God is our Savior. Only He can
free us. Only He can heal our broken hearts and spirits. We must not
forget our Savior as the Israelites did.[103]

This is the God we adore. The great and sovereign ruler of the universe who saves us from ourselves and from Satan.

Think About It:
Read **Psalm 106.21** in context. How do modern Christians sometimes
forget who is their Savior?

---

102   Ephesians 2.1-5
103   Psalm 106.21

✋ Hand in Hand

For the grace of God has appeared, bringing salvation for all people, training us to renounce ungodliness and worldly passions, and to live self-controlled, upright, and godly lives in the present age, waiting for our blessed hope, the appearing of the glory of our great God and Savior Jesus Christ, who gave himself for us to redeem us from all lawlessness and to purify for himself a people for his own possession who are zealous for good works.[104]

God did not save us so we could merely continue acting as we did before we became Christians. He did not save us so we could continue in sin and death. He saved us to set us free for righteousness. He saved us so we might turn away from ungodliness and our worldly passions. He saved us so we could pursue godliness, righteousness and self-control. He saved us so we could be zealous for good works. He saved us so we might look forward to the coming of Jesus Christ to take us home to heaven.

Sadly, some folks are not really looking forward to that. Sure, they want it. That is, they want it more than the alternative. They don't want to go to hell at the judgment. However, they really aren't awaiting the coming of Jesus. They hope the coming of Jesus delays because they are having too much fun in the world. Going to heaven would cramp their style. Certainly, if it comes right down to it, they hope God will usher them in when they no longer have a choice. For now, however, they want to pursue the things of the world. We must not live like this. Our lives must look forward to the coming of Jesus. We must not be attached to this world. We must not love the things of the world, they will only overthrow our souls.[105]

As Paul taught Titus how the saved should act if they wished to walk hand in hand with God the Savior in **Titus 3**, he mentioned some very specific things. He pointed out that we need to be submissive to our rulers and governing authorities. We need to follow everything from tax laws to speed limits. The saved submit to the government established by God.

We are "to speak evil of no one, to avoid quarreling, to be gentle, and to show perfect courtesy toward all people."[106] The saved need to speak

---

104	**Titus 2.11-14**
105	**I John 2.15-17**
106	**Titus 3.2**

like they are saved. We need to think the best of people and speak the best of them. We need to treat others gently, showing them courtesy. We are to steer clear of quarrels.

As we have said repeatedly throughout this study, we must devote ourselves to good works. That is, we must devote ourselves to the work for which the Scripture equips us.[107] As we focus on good works, we must refrain from foolish controversies based on speculations and personal conscience. No doubt, we must stand firm for the doctrine of Christ, but we must not make every small speculation of ours a doctrinal test of fellowship. If we stir up division, Paul says we are warped and sinful. The church is to avoid us. Rather than let the church be divided by us, the church is to divide from us if we are quarrelsome.[108]

If we want to walk hand in hand with God, the Savior, we must act like the saved. We must turn from all the sins from which God saved us. If we continue in it, we have forgotten our Savior and cannot hope for salvation. However, as we focus on Him and grow in good works, we can look forward to salvation in the end.

Think About It:

From what did God save you? What does that mean about how you should act toward those things now?

---

107   **Titus 3.1, 8; II Timothy 3.16-17**
108   **Titus 3.9-11**

Praying to Our God

Dear God, You are...

Dear God, You...

Dear God, thank You...

Dear God, forgive me for...

Dear God, help me...

$$\left(\ 15\ \right)$$

God, the Redeemer

Getting Our Bearings

If you address as Father the One who impartially judges according to each one's work, conduct yourselves in fear during the time of your stay on earth; knowing that you were not redeemed with perishable things like silver or gold from your futile way of life inherited from your forefathers, but with precious blood, as of a lamb unblemished and spotless, the blood of Christ.[109]

We often talk about Jesus as our Redeemer. We sing the song "The Great Redeemer." However, do we know the background behind redemption? Redemption was not mentioned in the New Testament in a vacuum. Rather, there were two very important Old Testament pictures brought to mind by this word.

Leviticus 25.47-50 gives us one picture. An Israelite, for one reason or another, had become poor. No longer able to provide for himself, he sold himself into slavery. He was no longer his own person. He was now his master's. Though many masters in this time may have been good to their slaves, it was still a pitiful state to be so poor one could only sell his life to another. Read **Nehemiah 5.1-5** to see how wretched this state of slavery often was to the Jews.

However, someone could come along and redeem the poor man from slavery. That is, he could pay the purchase price of the slave to the slave owner, prorated for the number of years the slave had left in servitude before the Year of Jubilee. What a great benefactor this redeemer was.

98

The redeemer paid the ransom price to release the slave from his bondage. God has done this for us. He has paid the ransom price that we might be set free from our slavery to sin and Satan.

That price was the precious blood of Jesus. No doubt if a man had to pay a few hundred, maybe even thousand, dollars to release his friend or relative from slavery he might. But sacrificing the blood of His Son? What a great price God paid to free us from slavery.

However, this is not the only picture of redemption. Perhaps a more fundamental picture is found in **Exodus 13**. God had freed Israel from Egypt with His final plague. He killed the firstborn of the Egyptians, from the Pharaoh to the captives in the dungeons and all the livestock. However, the firstborn of the Jews were protected. All who put the Passover blood on their door were protected from the plague.

However, the reality was the firstborn of the Israelites deserved death as much as those of Egypt. Something must be done about this. God came up with a plan of redemption. In **Exodus 13.1**, God said that all the firstborn of both man and beast belonged to Him. The firstborn of the livestock were to be sacrificed. Yet, God did not want human sacrifice. The firstborn among the men were to be redeemed. A redemption price was set in **Numbers 18.16** of five shekels of silver.

Our slavery was not just a matter of control. It was a matter of death. We were headed for eternal slaughter, spiritually. It is what we deserved. However, God paid the redemption price that kept us from being executed at His altar. Jesus paid that price by being the redeeming sacrifice. If we think about it, we are like the donkey whose neck was to be broken if it wasn't redeemed. However, if the owner wished to keep the donkey, he had to redeem it with the life of a lamb.[110] Jesus, the lamb of God, shed His blood that our necks need not be broken. Having been redeemed, we are now consecrated for holy use by the One who has paid the purchase price.

This is the God we adore. In order to save us from ourselves and our own sins, He paid the purchase price of blood, but not just any blood. He came into the world as one of us and paid with His own blood.

Think About It:
What do you think we could offer by way of payment to provide for our own redemption?

Hand in Hand

Oh give thanks to the Lord, for he is good, for his steadfast love endures forever! Let the redeemed of the Lord say so, whom he has redeemed from trouble and gathered in from the lands, from the east and from the west, from the north and from the south. Some wandered in desert wastes, finding no way to a city to dwell in; hungry and thirsty, their soul fainted within them. Then they cried to the Lord in their trouble, and he delivered them from their distress. He led them by a straight way till they reached a city to dwell in. Let them thank the Lord for his steadfast love, for his wondrous works to the children of man![111]

If we wish to walk hand in hand with God the Redeemer, we must be the redeemed who say so. We must acknowledge our redemption to God. We must thank God. Not just once, but continually. Is there any day in which we should not sing praise to God for setting us free from our enslavement and redeeming us from death?

However, I don't think this psalm is merely about acknowledging our redemption to our Redeemer. The redeemed must say so to others. We must acknowledge our redemption to our brothers and sisters. We must acknowledge our redemption to the world.

Peter said his audience was ransomed from the futile ways of their fathers. The Jewish Christians had inherited a system of Temple worship, priesthood and sacrifices that kept them burdened down in the minutia of constant law keeping. The Gentile Christians inherited a system of paganism trying to buy off their gods with money or sacrifice (sometimes even human). God had freed them from that. They should acknowledge that to their "fathers." They should let others know of their new found freedom in Christ.

Granted, we have not inherited the systems our spiritual forbearers had. However, the same principle applies to us. We should acknowledge what God has done for us. We must acknowledge this by abandoning our futile ways of the past and embracing the ways of God, even when our friends malign us for it.[112] We must acknowledge this by teaching them about this redemption. We need to pass the good news on to them. We need to stand up and say so.

What are we waiting for? Let us give thanks to our God. Let us sing His praises. Let us acknowledge His great love, mercy and redemption. If we truly believe it is such a great thing, why not tell others about it?

If we wish to walk hand in hand with God, the Redeemer, then let us stand up as the redeemed and say so. Let us acknowledge who we are and who God is.

Think About It:
To whom will you acknowledge your redemption this week? How will you do so?

Praying to Our God

Dear God, You are...

Dear God, You...

Dear God, thank You...

Dear God, forgive me for...

Dear God, help me...

Walking Together

What were the most important lessons you learned about God this week?

How did this week's readings help you walk closer to God?

What advice would you give others based on this week's reading to help them walk hand in hand with God?

With what issues do you need help or prayers based on this week's reading?

List some practical ways Christians can serve each other today following Christ's example of service?

What will our daily lives look like if we are living as a sacrifice for Jesus?

How should we relate to others if we are living as the saved?

How can we acknowledge our redemption to others this week?

Week Four
God of Love

"Anyone who does not love does not know God, because God is love. In this the love of God was made manifest among us, that God sent his only Son into the world, so that we might live through him. In this is love, not that we have loved God but that he loved us and sent his Son to be the propitiation for our sins."

I John 4.8-10

16

God, the Love

Getting Our Bearings

"God is love."[113]

The Romans had Cupid and Venus. The Greeks had Eros and Aphrodite. The Etruscans had Alpan, Turan and Uni. The Mesopotamians had Ishtar. The Canaanites had Anath. The Norse had Astrild, Freya and Sjofn. The Egyptians had Qadesh and Qetesh.[114]

In one way or another, each of these gods and goddesses were connected to love by the people who believed in them. Their special province was love. However, the gods and goddesses themselves may not always be very loving. They were like all the gods and goddesses of the pagans—fickle; their devotion had to be won by some merit of the men and women who called on them.

That is not our God. When John said, "God is love," he didn't mean God had some special province over love or some special attachment to those who love. He meant God is love. God's very nature is love.

No doubt, this boggles our minds. The God who is a consuming fire,[115] is also love. The God who brings judgment on sinners, loves those very sinners. We struggle to see how both can be true at the same time. Let's not struggle, let us merely accept what God says of Himself. However, this should really not be all that difficult to understand. In fact, it is very much like our parenting. I love my children very much. I imagine if you

---

113   **I John 4.8, 16**
114   www.godchecker.com
115   **Deuteronomy 4.24; Hebrews 12.29**

have children, you love them too. However, we discipline our children for their own good and when they rebel, we punish them. Why then is it so hard to understand our heavenly Father is at the same time a consuming fire and love?

John's point was to explain why God loves us. The pagan gods and goddesses loved their devotees because they were pretty, rich, smart or had offered good enough sacrifices. Jehovah God, however, loves us because He is love, because love is His very nature. Some parents love their children when they do well in school, when they are good at sports, when they are pretty or when they act just like the parent. But not our Heavenly Father. He loves us because He is love.

No matter our looks, wealth, health, strength, physical prowess or even holiness, God loves us. No doubt, God will not accept us if we sin without repentance. He will punish us because He is a consuming fire if we rebel, but all the while He loves us. We know that because **I John 4.9** says God sent His Son so we might live through Him. **Romans 5.6-8** says God sent His Son while we were ungodly, sinful enemies.

He did not accept us while sinfully rebellious. He did not just save us in our sins. He is a consuming fire. He couldn't abide with that. However, He is also love. Therefore, though we were rebellious, He sent His Son that we might have the means of salvation. That is love. Can you imagine providing the very means by which everyone who has ever hurt, betrayed or victimized you can be forgiven by you? That is God's love.

This is the God we adore. The creating ruler/judge who is a consuming fire is also love. Therefore, despite our rebellion He provided a way of escape from our rebellion so we might be saved and enjoy the benefits of His love.

Think About It:
Think of some other ways in which God has shown you love?

✋ Hand in Hand

If we are going to walk hand in hand with the God who is love, we need to remember that love. We need to remember God has displayed His love in no uncertain terms.

Sadly, too many Christians have been turned from God by the devil's lies. Satan wants us to believe God doesn't love us. One way of accomplishing this is to make us suffer. Job is one extreme example. Satan was sure if God moved the hedges of safety, Job would curse God. We can argue about whether or not Job ever sinned within the book; we can't, however, argue with the fact that Job never cursed God and up to the end, Job knew his salvation came from God. He knew who was His redeemer. He continued to hope in God even at his lowest.[116]

Paul addressed this issue in **Romans 8.35-39**: Who shall separate us from the love of Christ? Shall tribulation, or distress, or persecution, or famine, or nakedness, or danger, or sword? As it is written, 'For your sake we are being killed all the day long; we are regarded as sheep to be slaughtered.' No in all these things we are more than conquerors through him who loved us. For I am sure that neither death nor life, nor angels nor rulers, nor things present nor things to come, nor powers, nor height nor depth, nor anything else in all creation, will be able to separate us from the love of God in Christ Jesus our Lord.

This passage recognizes that Christians will face distress, persecution, famine and danger. We will get sick. Our loved ones get sick. We may get fired from our jobs. We may get hurt in accidents. We may get cancer, diabetes, heart disease. We may endure strokes, heart attacks and car wrecks. Enemies will attack us. Friends will betray us. Even our brethren will let us down. Satan has one goal in all this. He wants us to doubt God's love. He wants us to get upset with God and turn our back on Him.

We need to remember God has already shown His love and nothing else will change that. God doesn't have to heal our cancer to show His love for us. He doesn't have to steer our car away from a wreck to say He loves us. He doesn't have to find us a job when we first ask to demonstrate His love. He sent His Son to die for us while we were undeserving sinners. What more could He do to say, "I love you"?

---

116   **Job 13.15**

Do not let Satan block your view of Jesus on the cross. He will try. No matter what you face, look to Jesus. I believe this is one of the reasons the Bible indicates we should take the Lord's Supper every first day of the week. We need the constant reminder. God loves me this much. He loved me so much He shed His own Son's blood on the cross. He offered up His own Son's flesh as a sacrifice.

If we are going to walk hand in hand with God, we need to envision Jesus on that cross every day. We must not let Satan hinder that vision.

Think About It:
What is Satan putting in your life right now to make you think God doesn't love you?

How will you focus on God's love?

Praying to Our God

Dear God, You are…

Dear God, You…

Dear God, thank You…

Dear God, forgive me for…

Dear God, help me…

(17)

God, the Light

✦ Getting Our Bearings

"This is the message we have heard from him and proclaim to you, that God is light, and in him is no darkness at all."[117]

On the first day of creation, God said, "Let there be light." And it was so. However, the sun was not created until the fourth day. No doubt this dilemma causes great problems for many Bible students. How can there be light if there was no source of light, we ask? But there was a source. God Himself was the source. God is light.

Granted, that is mixing a metaphor with a reality. However, I believe those first few days of creation provide a great picture of God as light. Just as He was the source of light in a physical sense for the newly created world, He is the source of spiritual light for us even now.

Consider the pictures of **Isaiah 60.19-20** and **Revelation 21.23**. As God talked about His victorious children who basked in His glory, He presented a picture of cities needing no sun by day or moon by night. God was their light and the light never faded.

God is light and in Him is no darkness. This picture represents God's holiness. He is as a light so bright we cannot block it out. In His presence, we could close our eyes, but it would do no good. His light would pierce our eyes. His holiness is such that we sinful creatures could not even look upon it. In His presence, the only dark spot in the picture is us.

However, at times we feel encompassed by darkness. Perhaps we are facing trials and temptations. Perhaps we have already succumbed to the temptation and we fear we have gone too far. Perhaps we, at times, feel as David did in **Psalm 139.8** that we are making our bed in Sheol, the pit. In those cases, we have the great comfort David also had. "For it is you who light my lamp; the Lord my God lightens my darkness."[118]

God shines through the darkness and lights our path for us. God's light will lead us through our own darkness. "Send out your light and your truth; let them lead me."[119] God's leading light is His truth. His truth is His Word.[120] By spending time with God in His word our way is flooded with light. When we think Satan has us trapped and we cannot see the way through the darkness, we can turn to God and His Word. The light will shine through the darkness and show us the way like a lighthouse on the shore guiding us to safe harbor within the storm.

This is the God we adore. He *is* light. He is *the* light. He is *our* light. His holiness shines forth in unapproachable light and yet His light spreads through the darkness beckoning us to approach anyway.

Think About It:
Why is it important to you to know that God is Light and in Him is no darkness?

---

118   **Psalm 18.28**
119   **Psalm 43.3**
120   **John 17.17**

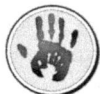

Hand in Hand

If we want to walk hand in hand with God the Light, we must walk in the light ourselves. "If we say we have fellowship with him while we walk in darkness, we lie and do not practice the truth."[121] We must walk in the light as He is in the light if we wish to be in fellowship with Him. This is of course the obvious point to make. Yet, we have made that same point over and over again in one way or another throughout our study. Let us, therefore, recognize another aspect of God's light.

If we wish to walk hand in hand with God the Light, we need to let His light spread to us. Do you remember Moses when he came down from his time with God on the mountain? His face shone from the glory of God.[122] The light of God was transferred to Moses as he walked with God and talked with Him. So bright was the light, Moses had to veil his face so the people would not be blinded.

We must allow a similar transfer in our lives. We have no light in ourselves. We have stamped it out with our own sin. God's light however can shine through us when we walk and talk with Him. Thus Jesus said of His kingdom citizens, "You are the light of the world."[123] We need to live so others can see our light, that is, God's light through us.

Jesus went on to say, "Let your light shine before others, so that they may see your good works and give glory to your Father who is in heaven."[124] We do not shine our light so people will see us. We shine our light so people may see God.

I love the song we sing, "Let the Lower Lights Be Burning." It tells the story well. Our Father is like the huge lighthouse shining out to warn the sailors of the dangerous rocks and to guide them to the safe harbor. We are like the little houses lining the shore that help guide the sailors as well.

By our light, some will see the safe harbor. "Keep your conduct among the Gentiles honorable, so that when they speak against you as evildoers, they may see your good deeds and glorify God on the day of visitation."[125] Thus, we learn we must let our light shine no matter how anyone responds.

---

121   I John 1.6
122   Exodus 34.29-35
123   Matthew 5.14
124   Matthew 5.16
125   I Peter 2.12

Allow me to warn you, being that shining light means you are a city set on a hill that cannot be hidden.[126] The enemies want to capture the city set on a hill because of its strategic location. You may want to hide from them, but you cannot. The same light that helps some glorify God, attracts the attention of those who hate the light because it exposes their evil deeds.[127]

If we want to walk hand in hand with God the Light, we must let His light shine through us whether it helps others glorify Him or attracts the attention of enemies.

Think About It:
How can you let your light shine today?

---

126 **Matthew 5.14**
127 **John 3.20**

(18)

God, the Provider

Getting Our Bearings

"Every good gift and every perfect gift is from above, coming down from the Father of lights with whom there is no variation or shadow due to change."[128]

"If you then who are evil, know how to give good gifts to your children, how much more will your Father who is in heaven give good things to those who ask him!"[129]

God's providence is a deep and sometimes confusing topic. Everyone has their own perspective on how it works. Let's refuse to be dragged into a debate on how it works, but merely accept the fact that it does work.

"Providence" is derived from the Latin word "providentia," which in turn combines two words "pro" (before) and "videre" (to see). Thus, the word literally meant "to see ahead" or "to see beforehand."[130] However, the concept of providence goes beyond merely seeing what is coming and further implies preparing for what is coming. We might define "providence" as God's foreseeing care and guardianship of His people. We can rest assured God provides for His people what they need. This is God's provide-ence.

"And we know that God causes all things to work together for good to those who love God, to those who are called according to His purpose."[131] God causes all things to work together for good. Notice it didn't say God causes all things. However, God, through His foreknowl-

128 James 1.17
129 Matthew 7.11
130 Cottrell, Jack, *What the Bible Says about God the Ruler*, Joplin, Missouri, 1984, p 9.
131 **Romans 8.28, NASU**

118

edge and foresight can weave even the most horrendous life experiences into a beautiful tapestry. He can even take a thorn in the flesh, a messenger of Satan, and use it to help us get to heaven.[132]

Acts 27.21-44 provides a great example of God's providence. An angel told Paul no one on the doomed ship would die. We know that physical salvation will come from God. He promised it. Yet, as we read the story and wait for the hand of God to miraculously save the ship, it never happens. As we wait for men to be plucked out of the water and set on dry land by the mighty hand of God, it never happens. However, amazingly, every single man on that ship, 276 in all, were able to either swim to shore or grab hold of the flotsam and float safely to land. Amazing! God provided for the lives of 276 men. His foreseeing care and guardianship gave some men the ability to swim and gave others a plank or other debris to which they could cling. God provided. Yet, when all the men were on shore, no one had seen God or even His mighty work. It all seemed to just take place naturally. But who can believe 276 men could all survive a shipwreck?

That is exactly what God does for us. He provides. Often we cannot even see how, but we know, by faith, God is the one providing. Consider another great example—the story of Esther. This book has been criticized because God never appears in the story. Yet, serious students can't help but see God everywhere.

It just happened that Ahasuerus needed a new queen. It just happened that Esther was available. It just happened that Esther was able to gain the favor of Hegai, the eunuch in charge of the maidens. It just happened that Esther was chosen to be the new queen. It just happened that Mordecai discovered a plot that saved the king's life. It just happened that the king couldn't sleep one night. It just happened that the record they brought to the king was of Mordacai's loyalty. It just happened that Esther was granted access to the king. And all of this just happened so Esther was uniquely placed to help her Jewish brethren at the same time as Haman had developed his plot to destroy the Jews. Can any of us really believe that all of this just happened? I can't.

We can't see God working. We don't know how He worked. However, is there any doubt God provided for His people? The same is true today.

We have food on our tables, clothes on our backs, roofs over our heads, brethren to support us and so much more. How did all of this happen? God provided. All of that providence comes together for one express purpose—to come together for the ultimate good of conforming us to the image of Christ so we may attain the resurrection to eternal life. As Paul said, "If while we were enemies we were reconciled to God by the death of his Son, much more, now that we are reconciled, shall we be saved by his life."[133]

This is the God we adore. He loves and provides for us that we might be reconciled to Him and that we might stay in Him, walking with Him on the path to heaven.

Think About It:
Can you think of any times in your life where you are sure God must have providentially played a part? List some below.

---

133   Romans 5.10

Hand in Hand

If we want to walk hand in hand with God the Provider, we must learn to trust God's ability to see the big picture. We must remember that God can see tomorrow and we can't.

Too often we spend our days worried about what will come and our nights fretting over tomorrow. However, "which of you by being anxious can add a single hour to his span of life?"[134] Instead, we must trust God, seek first His kingdom and righteousness and let Him provide for us.[135]

Matthew 7.9-11 says God wants to give us good gifts. When we ask for bread, He won't give us a stone. When we ask for a fish, He won't give us a snake. However, sometimes we are asking for the snake and the stone and we don't realize it. Other times God is giving us the fish and the bread and we are too immature to recognize it.

Who knew when Joseph was sold into slavery and then framed into prison, these turn of events would be his ticket to become second in command of all Egypt? Who knew that when Moses fled Egypt, afraid for his life, his 40 years in the wilderness would make him perfectly suited to be the leader God needed? Who knew when the new Pharaoh enslaved Israel, it would also provide the means to strengthen the people and the protection for them to grow into a mighty nation? Who knew when David's flock was attacked by lions and bears, it was preparing him to fight Goliath? Who knew when Ezekiel was being carried to captivity, it was preparing him to be a great prophet? Who knew when Jesus was being nailed to the cross, God was providing the sacrifice for our salvation?

Let's face it. We can't see the big picture. We have no idea what our life as a whole will look like when it is done. Therefore, we have no idea what scene today's mess will play in the symphony of our lives. Like a minor chord in a song, there seems to be some discord. However, when the whole piece is played, if we trust God, it will sound beautiful.

If you want to walk hand in hand with God the Provider, don't try to do His job. Don't try to make everything work out. Don't fret and worry about how it will all end. Simply do whatever you know is right, wherever you end up, with whoever you can and trust God to make it all work together for good.

---

134   **Matthew 6.27**
135   **Matthew 6.33**

Think About It:

Can you think of some bad things that happened in your life which you can now look back on to see that God worked them out for good? List them below.

Praying to Our God

Dear God, You are…

Dear God, You…

Dear God, thank You…

Dear God, forgive me for…

Dear God, help me…

19

God, the Shepherd

Getting Our Bearings

The Lord is my shepherd; I shall not want.
He makes me lie down in green pastures.
He leads me beside still waters.
He restores my soul.
He leads me in paths of righteousness for his name's sake.
Even though I walk through the valley of the shadow of death,
I will fear no evil,
for you are with me;
your rod and your staff,
they comfort me.
You prepare a table before me
in the presence of my enemies;
you anoint my head with oil;
my cup overflows.
Surely goodness and mercy shall follow me
all the days of my life,
and I shall dwell in the house of the Lord forever.[136]

Psalm 23 is perhaps one of the greatest expressions of God's love for us. No doubt, it is a little odd for us as modern urbanites. However, for David, a shepherd from youth, the picture of a shepherd with his sheep was stronger than the relationship of a boy with his dog like Travis and Old Yeller or Billy with Old Dan and Little Ann.[137]

---

136   **Psalm 23**
137   Though I did not research the book for this chapter and I don't quote it, I must admit my thoughts on **Psalm 23** are highly influenced by Phillip Keller's *A Shepherd Looks at Psalm 23*

Our Shepherd provides rest for us, giving us the comfort that allows us to lie down in the green pastures. Folks in the world can't rest, they have too much anxiety, too much worry. Someone else may get ahead of them. Someone may take advantage of them. We, however, following our Shepherd, can lie down and rest in peace and comfort.

We follow Him in His paths because He knows the way to the feeding grounds. We don't feel the need to get out of the fold at night and explore our own paths because we know our Shepherd and we wait for His voice.

When we are in the valley of the shadow of death, we do not fear because our protector is with us. Sadly, this passage is a mainstay of funeral messages even though it is not really about death. The valley of the shadow of death is not talking about when we die. It is about living and walking in the midst of enemies who might even try to kill us. The picture is not about facing cancer (though, I'm sure there is application). Rather, it is about working with the worldly who are trying to bring us down. It is about walking through life in the midst of the gossips, slanderers, backbiters, malicious, selfish people who prey on the innocent who live by godly standards. We have nothing to fear because our Shepherd is with us.

Like the sheep who get to the mountaintop tablelands prepared by the Shepherd, our God leads us to our spiritual feeding grounds. Though the predators look on from the edge of the feeding area, they fear to attack because of the Shepherd's watchful eye. He has cleared this feeding area of poisonous and harmful plants, leaving us free to feed.

He provides us with the salves and oils that keep away the bugs, ticks, worms that annoy and distract us, allowing us peace, contentment and comfort. He is always there to protect, guide, feed and comfort us.

This is the God we adore. He is our loving Shepherd. He draws us to Him and leads us in His paths of righteousness, protecting us along the way.

Think About It:

Why do you want to stay in the house of the Lord forever?

Hand in Hand

If we are going to walk hand in hand with God the Shepherd, we have to let Him be the leader. Jesus said,

> *He who enters by the door is the shepherd...The sheep hear his voice, and he calls his own sheep by name and leads them out. When he has brought out all his own, he goes before them, and the sheep follow him, for they know his voice.*[138]

We have to follow the voice of the Shepherd otherwise we aren't His sheep.

Most of us have seen the bumper sticker saying, "God is my co-pilot." Somebody thought they came up with a great little motto. However, I prefer the answering bumper sticker, "If God is your co-pilot, swap seats." The co-pilot is second in command. The captain is the one in charge and every choice the co-pilot makes must first be submitted to him. God should not be our co-pilot; He should be our Captain.

That means we need to do what He says submitting our choices to Him first. For instance, pretend for a moment one of your co-workers, friends, family members or brethren has done something to upset you. What should you do? We might be tempted to let it slide. After all, we don't want to rock the boat. It will be more trouble than its worth. I ask you, however, to think about how many relationships you don't have with people anymore because something upsetting happened and you did nothing about it. Resentment and bitterness built up. You began to view that relationship through the filter of the upsetting occurrence and eventually you no longer wanted to be around that person. When they asked if something was wrong, you probably told them no and explained how busy and distracted you were. Then eventually there was just no more relationship. Further, if the matter was sin, we have just allowed them to remain in that sin with all the consequences for their soul. We hate that when we look at it, but here we are doing the same thing with another person.

---

138   **John 10.2-4**

What might be different if we let God be our Shepherd? He says we must not allow our anger to linger. "Be angry and do not sin; do not let the sun go down on your anger, and give no opportunity to the devil."[139] He says we need to go to people if they have done something against us and talk to them about it. "If your brother sins against you, go and tell him his fault, between you and him alone. If he listens to you, you have gained your brother."[140]

God's directions scare us. We don't like them. We would rather live and let live. But be honest. It never really works that way. What would happen if we actually took the time to figure out a way to bring up our concerns, frustrations, even anger in a non-threatening, non-confrontational way and talk to the person? No doubt, some few people will blow up and end the relationship. However, most people will respond positively. In any event, you will have done whatever you could so that as much as it depends on you, you can be at peace with all people.[141]

This was just one practical example. I'm sure we could come up with dozens of times when our natural response is not God's response. If we are going to walk hand in hand with God the Shepherd, we are going to have to let Him take the lead.

Think About It:

What are some other scenarios where our natural response is not God's response? What is God's response in those situations?

Do you have any of those kinds of situations in your life now? If so, how can you correct them?

---

139   **Ephesians 4.26-27**
140   **Matthew 18.15**
141   **Romans 12.18**

Praying to Our God

Dear God, You are…

Dear God, You…

Dear God, thank You…

Dear God, forgive me for…

Dear God, help me…

20

God, the Listener

Getting Our Bearings

The Lord is at hand; do not be anxious about anything, but in everything by prayer and supplication with thanksgiving let your requests be made known to God. And the peace of God, which surpasses all understanding, will guard your hearts and minds in Christ Jesus.[142]

Humble yourselves, therefore, under the mighty hand of God so that at the proper time he may exalt you, casting all your anxieties on him, because he cares for you.[143]

If you know me, you know I am a talker. One of the dangers of being a talker is after a while, people get tired of listening. They tire because I am telling the same story for the fifteenth time. They tire because they have their own problems and are sick of hearing mine. They tire because what's important to me just isn't important to them. They tire because they are talkers too and let's face it, good talkers are rarely great listeners. Perhaps you have become tired of listening to some people or perhaps you have met people who were tired of listening to you.

God, however, never gets tired of listening. "Pray without ceasing," He said through Paul.[144] He wants us to pray. He wants to hear what we have to say. He wants to hear our feelings. He wants to hear our confessions. He wants to hear our praises. He wants to hear our pleas. He wants to hear our cries. His ear is always open. The Lord is always at hand.

---

142   **Philippians 4.5-7**
143   **I Peter 5.6-7**
144   **I Thessalonians 5.17**

One of the greatest messages of the **Psalms** as a whole is God's listening ear. Many of the psalms are prayers. Just read through them and notice to what God will listen.

No doubt, He never tires of listening to our praises of Him. Consider **Psalm 8**. "O Lord our Lord how majestic is Your name." However, God does not turn His ears only to the praises and away from everything else. God never tires of hearing our petitions. Consider **Psalm 16**. "Preserve me, O God, for in you I take refuge." **Psalm 17**, "Hear a just cause, O Lord; attend to my cry!" He never tires of hearing our confessions. Consider **Psalm 51**. "I know my transgressions, and my sin is ever before me. Against you, you only, have I sinned." Unlike some of our friends who start to get tired of us if we have repeat offenses, God is always there to listen and forgive when we confess and repent.

Most of us think God's listening stops there. However, are you aware God never tires of listening to our emotions about other people? There are some psalms that cause Christians great trouble. They are called imprecatory psalms. These are the psalms where God's child calls for destruction on his enemies. Consider some lines from **Psalm 109**: Appoint a wicked man against him; let an accuser stand at his right hand. When he is tried, let him come forth guilty; let his prayer be counted as sin! May his days be few; may another take his office! May his children be fatherless and his wife a widow! May his children wander about and beg, seeking food far from the ruins they inhabit! May the creditor seize all that he has; may strangers plunder the fruits of his toil!

As Christians, who are taught to love our enemies, we wonder how God can listen to this. How could this have ever been allowed? One thing we note, however, is David never treated any of his enemies this way. David refused to lift his hand against Saul. He tried every means to save the life of Absalom. What we see in these psalms is the inner turmoil of emotion against people. We, who too often let these feelings vent toward others, learn from David where we should take them. We should take them to God. He never tires of listening. He will listen as we vent that anger and frustration. Then we can leave the action up to Him, knowing He will do what is right.

Even more shocking, however, is God will even listen as we vent frustrations with Him. **Psalm 88** has always intrigued me. Heman the Ezrahite had a bad life. The psalm begins bad, the middle is bad and in the end, things are still bad. Further, Heman blamed God. He railed against God and begged Him to do something about how bad things were. He said he had cried out to God every day about this. We see one psalm, but God listened to this prayer over and again. God is the great provider who sees the big picture. However, He is also the all-wise God who knows we can't see the big picture. He knows we get frustrated, perhaps even angry, because we can't see all ends. He will listen even when we are upset with Him. However, we must keep in mind what He-man did. He continued to rely on God, knowing salvation comes from Him. If we are upset, we may take that to God in prayer, but we must not turn from God because of it. He is still God.

This is the God we adore. He is a listener. His line is always open. He is always at hand for whatever we want to talk about.

Think About It:
Is there anything you haven't taken to God in prayer? Do it now.

Hand in Hand

Do I even need to write down what we must do on a practical level every day if we want to walk hand in hand with God the Listener? Surely, you have already figured it out.

We must pray.

We must not pray little rote prayers. "God is great, God is good, let us thank Him for our food." We must not pray as a mantra to manipulate God, for instance repeating the prayer of Jabez as if merely repeating the words has any value. We need to pray from the heart. We need to pray what is on our minds.

We need to adore God and tell Him why. We need to appreciate God for His blessings and give Him thanks. We need to recognize our own unworthiness before God and confess our sins. We need to depend on God and petition Him for His care and guardianship.

We need to seek His strength every day. Paul said, "We do not wrestle against flesh and blood, but against the rulers, against the authorities, against the cosmic powers over this present darkness, against the spiritual forces of evil in the heavenly places."[145] We do not pray because God has required it. We pray because we are wrestling with an enemy we can't beat. Satan is too strong for us and he is stalking us.

If we hope to remotely beat Satan or escape his traps, we have to pray. We have to connect to God that God's power might flow through us. Remember, God is "able to do far more abundantly than all we ask or think, according to the power at work within us."[146]

Not only must we pray, if we want to walk hand in hand with God the Listener, we must also be willing to listen ourselves. In **Isaiah 66.3-4** God said the Israelites who had sacrificed oxen and lambs were like those who had sacrificed humans; that is, their worship was repugnant to Him. Why? Because they had chosen their own way over His. Instead of listening to God's word and God's laws, they had followed their own path. They refused to listen to God, yet, they expected God to listen to them when they came to worship Him. It doesn't work that way.

---

145   Ephesians 6.12
146   Ephesians 3.20

If we want God to listen to us, we had better listen to His Word. Our sins will separate us from God.[147] He does not becomes tired of listening, rather, He longs to listen. That is why He sent His Son so we might be reconciled to Him. Yet, if we give ourselves to sin, He simply will not listen. If we turn our back on Him, He will not turn His ear to us until we come confessing and repenting. Then, no matter how bad we have been, He is the Father of the Prodigal who comes racing out to meet us so He can listen to us again.[148]

What a great God we have who will listen to us. Have you been speaking to Him? Have you been listening to Him? When was the last time?

Think About It:
Before you move to the prayer exercise on the next page, are there any Bible passages to which you know you haven't listened? If so, what are they and how can you make reconciliation?

---

147   **Isaiah 59.1-2**
148   **Luke 15.20**

Praying to Our God

Dear God, You are…

Dear God, You…

Dear God, thank You…

Dear God, forgive me for…

Dear God, help me…

Walking Together

What were the most important lessons you learned about God this week?

How did this week's readings help you walk closer to God?

What advice would you give others based on this week's reading to help them walk hand in hand with God?

With what issues do you need help or prayers based on this week's reading?

How has God demonstrated His love to you?

What advice would you give for others about letting their light shine to help people in the world glorify God?

When are some times you are convinced God has been working in your life for things to come out for good? Think especially of times when you thought the situation was bad, but it worked out for good in the end.

When are some times our natural response to a situation is not God's response and how do we pursue God's way?

WEEK FIVE
God is Good

"Or which one of you, if his son asks him for bread, will give him a stone? Or if he asks for a fish, will give him a serpent? If you then, who are evil, know how to give good gifts to your children, how much more will your Father who is in heaven give good things to those who ask him!"

Matthew 7.9-11

(21)

God, the Everpresent

Keep your life free from love of money, and be content with what you have, for he has said, 'I will never leave you nor forsake you.' So we can confidently say, 'The Lord is my helper; I will not fear; what can man do to me?'"[149]

Imagine what Ezekiel thought when he was taken captive, removed from his homeland and carried thousands of miles to Babylon. I wonder how many times he bemoaned that he would not be allowed to come into God's presence in the Jerusalem temple because he was so far away. I wonder if he ever felt like he was not only far away from the temple, but far away from God.

However, in a blaze of glory, the cherubim-carried throne of God burst into Ezekiel's life by the side of the river Chebar.[150] Ezekiel received a profound lesson that God is everpresent. God is not bound to one location. God doesn't have to travel to visit all His children all over the world. God is everywhere.

In **I Kings 18**, Elijah had a contest with the prophets of Baal. They were supposed to call on Baal and ask him to light their altar. When they hollered and yelled for hours, Elijah said, "Cry aloud, for he is a god. Either he is musing, or he is relieving himself, or he is on a journey, or perhaps he is asleep and must be awakened."[151] This statement provides a great contrast to what Elijah believed about Jehovah God.

---

149   **Hebrews 13.5-6**
150   **Ezekiel 1**
151   **I Kings 18.27**

140

Our God doesn't go on journeys. He is everywhere. He can hear me when I pray in Franklin, Tennessee and at the same time, hear you pray wherever you are. God is always at hand,[152] which is why we can cast our cares on Him no matter where we are.

Further, there is no danger of us losing God. Without getting into a debate on guardian angels, I have seen the bumper sticker that says, "Don't drive faster than your guardian angel can fly." That suggests we might go too fast for God and He can't keep up with us. That just can't happen. We can't get away from Him and Satan can't block us from Him. David drove this home in **Psalm 139.7-12**:

Where shall I go from your Spirit? Or where shall I flee from your presence? If I ascend to heaven, you are there! If I make my bed in Sheol, you are there! If I take the wings of the morning and dwell in the uttermost parts of the sea, even there your hand shall lead me, and your right hand shall hold me. If I say, "Surely the darkness shall cover me, and the light about me be night," even the darkness is not dark to you; the night is bright as the day, for darkness is as light with you.

This is the everpresent God we adore. Though our hectic lives lead us all over the globe, God is there. Though Satan tries to cover us with his cloak of darkness, God is there. Whether we are home or abroad, our God is with us. He will never forsake us.

Think About It:

What comfort do you gain from knowing God is with you all the time?

Hand in Hand

Interestingly, when the Hebrew writer wanted us to know God was with us always in **Hebrews 13.5-6**, he warned us not to be filled with the love of money. If we want to walk hand in hand with God the Everpresent, we need to place our faith and hope in Him.

Too many place their faith and hope in other things. No doubt, they believe God is the one who will let them into heaven and they look forward to that (they hope). However, when they get down to the meat and potatoes of life, all that "God stuff" is just pie in the sky. They want something more substantial, something they can put their hands on.

This is an age old problem. In fact, we see the same problem in **Exodus 32**. When the newly freed Israelites were separated from Moses who had been able to rally them to the unseen God, they wanted something more substantial, something they could see and touch. They made a calf and frolicked before it, acting as if the calf was Jehovah who had freed them.

We may not bow before golden calves or silver statues today, however we can be just as guilty. When we trust in money, material possessions, health, personal strength, family connections or political power to take care of us, then we have forsaken our God.

God is with us. He has promised to never forsake us. No matter where we are in the world or what stage we are in life, God is there. He will care for us. **Matthew 6.33** says, "Seek first the kingdom of God and his righteousness, and all these things will be added to you." God has promised to provide for us. God has promised to take care of us.

No doubt, God has never promised to plop us in the lap of luxury. He has never promised to lead us to new heights of individual fame and glory. Maybe that is why so many struggle with trusting God. However, He has promised to care and provide.

We need to remember that the greatest gain doesn't come from climbing the ladder of earthly success. The greatest gain comes from godliness with contentment.[153]

If we wish to walk hand in hand with God, we need to be content with His presence, putting our faith and hope for today, for tomorrow and for eternity in Him.

142

Think About It:

Why is it such a struggle to keep our daily hope and faith in God? What can we do to keep the proper focus?

Praying to Our God

Dear God, You are...

Dear God, You...

Dear God, thank You...

Dear God, forgive me for...

Dear God, help me...

㉒

God, the Challenger

✴ Getting Our Bearings

For this very reason, make every effort to supplement you faith with virtue, and virtue with knowledge, and knowledge with self-control, and self-control with steadfastness, and steadfastness with godliness, and godliness with brotherly affection, and brotherly affection with love. For if these qualities are yours and are increasing, they keep you from being ineffective or unfruitful in the knowledge of our Lord Jesus Christ.[154]

Through faith we have become God's children. He has wiped the slate clean for us, making us righteous. However, God is not done with us. He wants us to grow. We cannot stop with faith, we must have virtue, or as the New American Standard translates it, moral excellence. However, that is not enough, we must also have knowledge. Yet we can't stop there, we must have self-control. Do you see where this is heading?

Someone once said God's grace is so amazing it will accept us just as we are. However, His love is so profound He will not leave us that way. God pushes us to grow. He wants us to be better, to be more and more like Him.

Romans 6 demonstrates once we are God's children, we cannot merely continue to live the way we did before. We are dead to sin and alive to God. He wants us to live differently. However, this change is not natural. If we act naturally, we will continue to live as we did when we were by nature children of wrath.[155] There is no word for this change but challenge.

---

154   **II Peter 1.5-8**
155   **Ephesians 2.3**

God does not sit idly by and let us wile away the hours, stagnating in Christ. He is challenging us. He is throwing down the gauntlet and telling us to buck up and grow.

Look through history. God challenged Adam and Eve when He placed the tree of knowledge of good and evil in the garden. They failed. God challenged Cain when He told him to do well or sin would control him. He failed. God challenged Noah when He told him to build an ark. He succeeded. God challenged Abraham when He told him to go into a strange land. He succeeded. God challenged Moses when He told him to go to Pharaoh and demand that he let the people go. He succeeded. God challenged the prophets when He told them to speak in His name. Some succeeded. God challenged Peter when He told him to feed his sheep. He succeeded. God challenged Paul when He told him to be an apostle to the Gentiles. He succeeded.

Do we really think we can be any different? Do we really think God is happy to let us daydream our way into heaven, half-heartedly obeying Him when it is convenient? Do we really think we are right with God if we loaf in His fields instead of work in His vineyards?

God is challenging us. He is challenging us to put the passions of our flesh to death. He is challenging us to take His message to other people. He is challenging us to bear the fruit of His Spirit. He is challenging us to get out of our comfort zones. He is challenging us to be better Christians tomorrow than we are today.

This is the God we adore. Yes, His grace is so amazing He has accepted us the way we are. However, He is a challenger who will not rest until we are better tomorrow.

Think About It:

What challenges are you facing based on God's word right now?

Hand in Hand

If we are going to walk hand in hand with God the Challenger, we have to step up to the plate and accept the challenges. We have to roll up our sleeves and get to work.

There is only one way to face a challenge—one step at a time. However, before you take the first step, you need to formulate your goal. What exactly is the challenge you are facing and what must you have done to face up to the challenge?

For instance, God says we need to increase in knowledge. Obviously, we will never have all knowledge of God's will. There will always be room to grow. So you need to establish interim goals that demonstrate growth in knowledge. You might begin with the goal of knowing all the books of the Bible and their themes. You might progress with picking out one book at a time to learn its outline and then progress through them all. Then you may want to start with one book at a time and be able to list the theme of each chapter and then progress through all the others. I think you can agree that even this very simple approach will take you a long time. And above all, I think you can see that this is a challenge.

Perhaps you want to face the challenge of teaching someone the gospel. Begin by considering what convinced you to obey. Then think about what you need to know to teach someone. Develop a plan to teach them. Then you have to consider how to get to teach someone. You have to work on goals of bringing up spiritual conversations, making invitations, feeling out your prospects, etc. Will you go door knocking? Will you strike up conversations in Wal-Mart? Will you approach bank tellers? Will you talk with co-workers? Will you invite neighbors into your home? Will you have a regular study in your home? You need to work on the step-by-step process of contacting, broaching the subject, leading the study with people.

Perhaps the hardest part is that God is not literally in our faces pushing us. I remember being on the rowing squad in college. When we were in regattas or even in individual erg[156] tests, we had coaches and teammates in our faces yelling encouragement and shouting challenges. These spurred us on. God has given the Word, but even then He is not in our face to keep us in the Word every day. God intends to use His children

---

156   An ergometer was the rowing machine on which we practiced.

to keep us challenged. "Let us consider how to stir up one another to love and good works."[157] We need to find someone who will stay with us and stir us up. Further, we need to find someone to stir up. We are the vehicles of God's challenges and we need to be willing to be at both ends of the challenge spectrum.

Finally, we must be ready to fail sometimes. Everyone fails. Look at all those we listed as being challenged in the Bible in the first half of this chapter. Every one of them failed at some time. Noah got drunk. Abraham doubted God's plan. Moses killed a man and struck the rock. Peter denied Jesus. Paul had been a persecutor and a coveter. Yet, they all went on to serve the Lord. I can't help but think of Cain in that list. He had already failed once by offering a sacrifice without faith. However, God did not cut him off. He told him to learn from his mistake. If he had learned from his mistake, he could have gone on to great service. He didn't learn; he just increased his failure.

We must be prepared to fail. Then we must examine our failures and learn from them. Then we must forget the past and press on for the goal, straining forward for the prize that is in Christ Jesus.[158]

If we wish to walk hand in hand with God the Challenger, we must step up to the challenges and face them one step at a time. Never forget, while God is the challenger He is also our strength. If we rely on Him we will overcome the challenges. He doesn't allow us to be tempted beyond what we are able to handle,[159] which means He never allows the challenges to be too great. We can make it.

Think About It:
List a plan to face the challenges you listed in the previous section.

---

157   **Hebrews 10.24**

158   **Philippians 3.13-14**

159   **I Corinthians 10.13**

23

God, the Liberator

Getting Our Bearings

"Wretched man that I am! Who will deliver me from this body of death? Thanks be to God through Jesus Christ our Lord!"[160]

One of the greatest Bible stories is the Exodus. Israel had been in Egypt for hundreds of years. They had become slaves and their burden was great. They cried out to God for relief. God sent Moses and the Ten Plagues. When God was finished with Pharaoh and Egypt, they begged Israel to leave. However, Pharaoh thought better of it and hunted Israel down. Caught between the devil and the deep Red Sea, Israel thought their number was up, but, God had different plans. He divided the waters of the Red Sea, allowing the Israelites to pass through unscathed and then brought the water crashing down on the Egyptians. God liberated the Israelites by His great hand.

God is a liberator. He is our liberator.

II Timothy 2.22-24 talks about the enemies of Christ as those who are held captive by Satan. That is exactly where we have been, held captive. By the blood of Jesus, God has liberated us from Satan.

However, some Christians still live in captivity. They are held captive by fear, anxiety, addictive sin, depression, doubt, etc. They want to grow in Christ but they keep facing these obstacles. That is exactly what Paul talked about in **Romans 7**. He had been held captive by covetousness. He knew of only one way to overcome. Jesus Christ must deliver him.

Jesus did. By the time Paul wrote **Philippians,** he was able to say, "I have learned in whatever situation I am to be content."[161] Notice, Paul learned. He was not always content, but he learned contentment. God delivered him from his sin, not just delivering him from the guilt of it, but delivering him from the captivity and control of it.

Whatever you are facing, God can set you free. In fact, if you love God He will set you free. He has predestined that those who love Him will be conformed to the image of Jesus.[162] We can't help it. If we love God, He will work everything out so we are set free from all our captivities and conformed to Jesus' image until that day we are set free from this earthly captivity and finally set free in heaven.

Finally, Paul said, "God is faithful, and he will not let you be tempted beyond your ability, but with the temptation he will also provide the way of escape, that you may be able to endure it."[163] Additionally, Peter wrote, "The Lord knows how to rescue the godly from trials, and to keep the unrighteous under punishment until the day of judgment."[164] God knows how to liberate us from temptation and deliver us from Satan's snares. No wonder Jesus said we should pray, "Lead us not into temptation, but deliver us from evil."[165] That doesn't mean we will never be tempted. It merely means that when we rely on God, He will deliver us from our temptations. He is a liberator.

This is the God we adore. He is our leader and guide, carrying us on dry land through the Red Sea then on through the wilderness to the Promised Land.

Think About It:
Is anything holding you captive right now? If so, list it below.

161   Philippians 4.11
162   Romans 8.28-29
163   I Corinthians 10.13
164   II Peter 2.9
165   Matthew 6.13

Hand in Hand

What we have said so far is really about a dime a dozen. Everyone tells us God is our liberator and we should just trust Him. However, few tell us how to actually do that. What does this mean when it comes down to brass tacks?

If we want to walk hand in hand with God the Liberator, the first thing we must do is realize we cannot free ourselves from anything. Only the poor in spirit are liberated in the kingdom of heaven.[166] That is, only those who realize how weak they are, who realize they can do nothing to liberate themselves are freed. Only these will ever be meek enough to do whatever God tells them.

How many formulaic movies have we seen where the good guys are in a plane and the bad guys have killed the pilot. In the end, the good guys have won, but they somehow have to land the plane. What would happen if someone on the plane said, "Hey, I've got this; I'm pretty smart. Just move out of my way, I don't need any help"? They would likely crash. Usually, everyone on the plane knows how weak they are. They know if they try it on their own, they are going to die. What do they do? They put on the headset and do exactly what they are told by the pilot in the control tower. That is how we must live if we want to walk with the Liberator. We have to do exactly what He says.

After recognizing we cannot free ourselves and only God can free us, we need to be completely honest about what is holding us captive. We need to fearlessly and honestly examine our lives in order to confess to God where Satan still has a foothold. We need to turn each captivity over to God, letting him have control over each one, doing exactly what He says to do.

We must never act like we have completely beaten any of the areas in which Satan has held us captive. When we do that, Satan can sneak in and lay his traps again. As Paul said, "Let anyone who thinks he stands take heed lest he fall."[167] When we think we are standing, we easily forget we are only standing by God's strength and Satan has an open door. Therefore, we must maintain vigilance every day.

---

166   Matthew 5.3
167   I Corinthians 10.12

As we noted in the last chapter, in order to accomplish this, we need to get help from others. God works through His children. We need to find other Christians to whom we can confess our captivities. As James said, "Confess your sins to one another and pray for one another, that you may be healed."[168]

If we wish to walk hand in hand with God the Liberator, we have to let Him be the Liberator. If we keep thinking we can pull it off with only minimal help, we will always be enslaved. However, when we turn completely to Him, praise God, He will set us free.

Think About It:
Who can you turn to for help with your captivities?

What help do you need from them?

When will you talk to them about it?

24

God, the Mighty Fortress

Getting Our Bearings

The Lord is my rock and my fortress and my deliverer, my God, my rock, in whom I take refuge, my shield, and the horn of my salvation, my stronghold. I will call upon the Lord, who is worthy to be praised, and I am saved from my enemies.[169]

The heading of this psalm says David wrote it on the day the Lord rescued him from all his enemies, including Saul. When someone like David claims God is his fortress, we need to listen. He was a warrior. He slew Goliath and then became a leader of men. He carried even the rag-tag into battle and they became valiant warriors who won victories. Yet, David said it was God who was his fortress, his refuge, his protector.

God wants to be our mighty fortress. He wants to be our impregnable refuge. He wants to be the one to whom we turn for safety. The psalms are filled with praises of God's protection. **Psalm 61.2-3** says, "Lead me to the rock that is higher than I, for you have been my refuge, a strong tower against the enemy." **Psalm 144.2** says, "He is my steadfast love and my fortress, my stronghold and my deliverer, my shield and he in whom I take refuge, who subdues peoples under me." Even the **Proverbs** makes this same claim. **Proverbs 18.10** says, "The name of the Lord is a strong tower; the righteous man runs into it and is safe."

David did not believe his army was his refuge. He did not trust in horses and weapons. He trusted in God. Therefore, when, in youth, he faced Goliath, he was willing to stand against him with only a sling for a weapon. God was his fortress, how could Goliath hurt him? As he progressed to be the king who commanded armies, he never forgot armies did not win wars. God won wars. Armies did not keep his kingdom safe. God kept his kingdom safe.

God wants to be that same mighty tower and fortress for us. He wants to be our rock and our deliverer. He wants to be the one who protects us from our enemies. He can do that. God can overcome the enemies who seek to shoot us down on the job. He can protect and preserve us from the enemies who seek to slander us before the world. He can even protect and preserve us from our ultimate enemy, Satan.

However, let us make sure we learn from David. Letting God be our fortress does not mean bad things will never happen. God was David's fortress even while he fled from Saul in the wilderness and even while hidden among the Philistines. God was David's fortress even as he fled Jerusalem before his son, Absalom. Having God as our mighty fortress does not mean bad things will never happen. It means we will always endure the bad things through God's protection and be delivered from them by God's power. And if we are not delivered from them in life, then we will be delivered from them by death as the angels carry us away to Abraham's bosom for comfort and peace.

This is the God we adore. He is a strong and mighty fortress that cannot be assailed by anything Satan hurls at Him. He is the rock that cannot be broken. He is the refuge that cannot be penetrated, the shield that cannot be overcome.

Think About It:
List some times when you believe God has protected you from harm, physically, emotionally or spiritually?

🖐 Hand in Hand

If we are going to walk hand in hand with God the Mighty Fortress, we have to follow the example of David. We have to let God fight our battles.

Perhaps the greatest example is in the fight against Saul. David recognized Saul as the king of Israel. He refused to lay a finger on Saul, yet somehow he needed to be delivered from him. He let God fight the battle. David even had Saul within his grasp twice. He could have killed him outright as his men encouraged him, but he did not, choosing to let God deal with Saul in His time.[170]

We have no right to vengeance:

> *Beloved, never avenge yourselves, but leave it to the wrath of God, for it is written, "Vengeance is mine, I will repay, says the Lord." To the contrary, "if your enemy is hungry, feed him; if he is thirsty, give him something to drink; for by so doing you will heap burning coals on his head." Do not be overcome by evil, but overcome evil with good.[171]*

Peter said Christ was our example:

> *For to this you have been called, because Christ also suffered for you, leaving you an example, so that you might follow in his steps. He committed no sin, neither was deceit found in his mouth. When he was reviled, he did not revile in return; when he suffered, he did not threaten, but continued entrusting himself to him who judges justly.[172]*

Peter later brought this example home to us, saying, "Therefore let those who suffer according to God's will entrust their souls to a faithful Creator while doing good."[173] His point is that while we suffer, we entrust ourselves to God. If it is His will, He will protect us. If not, He will see us through the suffering. If not, He will deliver us to heaven. It is not up to us to make sure others get punished for their sins, not even for their sins against us. Rather, we entrust that to God. He will decide if vengeance or punishment is needed. We must trust Him to do right.

170	**I Samuel 24.1-7; 26.7-12**
171	**Romans 12.19-21**
172	**I Peter 2.21-23**
173	**I Peter 4.19**

When neighbors slander us, we do not slander in return. When co-workers betray us, we do not betray them in return. When family members hurt us, we do not hurt them in return. Rather, we do good to those who have hurt us and let God be the judge and avenger. We turn to Him for comfort and safety and trust His judgment.

Do not misunderstand. This does not deny that we must go to others when they have sinned against us to help them repent.[174] However, our goal is not to punish or seek vengeance. Our goal is not to put them in their place. Our goal is not to prove to them how right we are and how wrong they are. Our goal is to help them overcome their sin.

If we want to walk hand in hand with God the Mighty Fortress, we have to leave vengeance and punishment up to Him. We have to let Him fight the battles while we merely do what He has commanded of us.

Think About It:
Why do we often struggle to let God be the one who punishes and seeks vengeance on those who hurt us?

---

174   Matthew 18.15

Praying to Our God

Dear God, You are…

Dear God, You…

Dear God, thank You…

Dear God, forgive me for…

Dear God, help me…

25

God is So Good

 ## Getting Our Bearings

And as he was setting out on his journey, a man ran up and knelt before him and asked him, "Good Teacher, what must I do to inherit eternal life?"

And Jesus said to Him, "Why do you call me good? No one is good except God alone."[175]

What a month we have had. If there is one thing we have learned with every reading, with every walk, God is good. God is so good. God is so good. God is so good. He's so good to us.

He is good because He created us with everything we needed to live. He is good because the creation He made was good. He is good because He rules well as a servant and not as a despot. He is good because He judges righteously. He is good because Father, Son and Holy Spirit work together in perfect harmony to accomplish our salvation, which we do not deserve. He is good because Jesus came into the world to live as one of us, to serve us as our sacrificial Savior. He is good because He paid the price to redeem us. He is good because He loves us, casting His light so we might see the way. He is good because He, through His foreseeing care and guardianship over us, provides for us. He is good because He shepherds us in paths of righteousness, feeding us, caring for us, protecting us. He is good because He cares so much for us that He never tires of listening. He is good because He has promised to never forsake us. He is good because He is not willing to let us remain where we are, but challenges us to move forward, to press on for the goal. He is good because He has set us free from the guilt of our sin and continues to work to set us free from anything that holds us captive. He is good because He is our refuge, an everpresent shelter in the time of storm.

God is so good. What else is there to say? He is so good everyone else pales in comparison. That was Jesus' point in **Matthew 7.11** when He said, "If you then, who are evil, know how to give good gifts to your children, how much more will your Father who is in heaven give good things to those who ask him!" That was His point when He challenged the rich young ruler who called Him a good teacher. Ultimately, God is good and the rest of us just don't measure up. That is why we need Him so badly. That is why we need His grace.

God is good and His work toward us is good. "Every good and perfect gift is from above, coming down from the Father of lights with whom there is no variation or shadow due to change."[176] As we have said before, we can't always see the big picture. Sometimes we think the gifts we are receiving aren't so good. However, we can trust God. When all is said and done, we will be able to look back and see His goodness.

This is the God we adore. He is good beyond measure. Not because of who we want Him to be. He is good beyond measure because of who He is. Aren't you glad He is our God?

Think About It:
What good things has God done for you?

Hand in Hand

If we are going to walk hand in hand with our God who is good, we need to strive to be like Him. "But as he who called you is holy, you also be holy in all your conduct, since it is written, 'You shall be holy for I am holy.'"[177]

There is only one way to gain this holiness. Get in God's word, suit up in God's armor, pray for God's strength and then take the devil head on. Our month of exercise is over, but the fight is continuing. Keep your armor on and keep fighting. Have you ever noticed how much of the armor is actually tied to the Word of God?

Ephesians 6.14-17 speaks of the sword of the Spirit which is the Word of God, but is that the only part the Word plays in this armor? No. We must fasten on the belt of truth. **John 17.17** says God's Word is truth. We must put on the breastplate of righteousness. **II Timothy 3.16** says the Scripture trains us in righteousness. We shod our feet with the preparation of the gospel of peace. **Colossians 1.5** says the Word of Truth is the gospel. We must take up the shield of faith. **Romans 10.17** says faith comes by hearing the Word of God. Finally, we must put on the helmet of salvation. **II Timothy 3.15** says the Scriptures make us wise for salvation. There is only one way to continue walking with God. Stay in God's Word.

Your walks based on this book are finished now. I hope they have been beneficial. However, most of all, I hope these walks have developed a habit within you. I hope you continue walking with God each day. Open up His Word. Drink in the words of eternal life. Stretch out your hand and grasp God's. He will lead you. He will guide you. He will carry you when the way gets rough. He will challenge you when you slack too much. He will love you all the way.

He is a good God.

Think About It:
What will you start reading in your Bible in order to keep walking with God next week?

---

177   I Peter 1.15-16

Praying to Our God

Dear God, You are…

Dear God, You…

Dear God, thank You…

Dear God, forgive me for…

Dear God, help me…

Walking Together

What were the most important lessons you learned about God this week?

How did this week's readings help you walk closer to God?

What advice would you give others based on this week's reading to help them walk hand in hand with God?

With what issues do you need help or prayers based on this week's reading?

What comfort do you gain from God's everpresence?

Why is it important to accept and face God's challenges?

From what has God liberated you and when has He provided you with safety as a mighty fortress?

What good has God done for you?

Appendix

At the end of each daily walk, I have provided an outline to help you develop your own prayer based on what you have learned about God. Most of the outline is pretty self-explanatory. However, some parts might need a little explanation.

Complete each phrase in the outline with a statement or thought inspired by what you read on that particular day. Obviously, when you pray you can do so for whatever you want. However, to get the most out of each day's reading, focus the prayer outline on thoughts inspired from that reading.

Complete the phrase "Dear God, You are…" with thoughts about God's nature, who and what He is. For instance, "Dear God, You are the creator."

Complete the phrase "Dear God, You…" with thoughts about what God has done or is doing. For instance, "Dear God, You created the universe."

Complete the phrase "Dear God, thank You…" with thoughts of appreciation for what God has done. For instance, "Dear God, thank you for creating such a beautiful world."

Complete the phrase "Dear God, forgive me for…" with statements of confession. For instance, "Dear God, forgive me for misusing and abusing your good creation."

Complete the phrase "Dear God, help…" with petitions for God's strength and assistance. For instance, "Dear God, help me use what you have created wisely without beginning to worship the creation instead of You, the Creator."

This outline is a great tool and I want to give credit where credit is due. I adapted this from a sermon I heard by David Banning, a gospel preacher in Beaumont, Texas and author of the *Get Them Talking*[178] curriculum for junior high and high school students. I believe he heard about it from the creators of *Our Spiritual Heritage*[179] a Bible class curriculum for younger students.

---

178   www.getthemtalking.com
179   www.ourspiritualheritage.com

For a full listing of DeWard Publishing
Company books, visit our website:

www.deward.com